GW01237579

OF PEATS AND PUTTS CONTINENTAL

OF PEATS AND PUTTS CONTINENTAL

EXPLORING WHISKY AND GOLF ACROSS EUROPE

ANDREW BROWN

YOUCAXTON PUBLICATIONS

ISBN 978-1-914424-81-6

Published by YouCaxton Publications 2022

YouCaxton Publications
www.youcaxton.co.uk

For Fran, Eduardo, Magnus, Christian, Agnes, Hans, Patrick, Geoff, Lena, Mikael, Niels, Lars, Johann, Henrik, Anya, Roar, Trude, Petter Inge and Jerry and many other fellow golf and/or whisky enthusiasts whom I was privileged to meet on my travels.

Author's Note

THROUGHOUT THE BOOK, I refer to golf-course rankings; e.g. a particular course is ranked 'within the country's top ten'. There are many such rankings published often by golf magazines and websites and they obviously change over time. None is right and none is wrong as they are all subjective and different rankings apply different weights to certain criteria. They do, however, provide a broad guide to a particular course's quality. For ease in this book when I quote rankings, I am referring to the website Top100 golf courses.com at the time of writing. Whether a particular course is ranked, for example, 4th of 6th is not very important – I simply want to portray a broad impression of its relative merit

Other books in the series

Of Peats and Putts – A Whisky and Golf Tour of Scotland

Mashies and Mash-Tuns – A Whisky and Golf Tour of England, Wales and Ireland

Of Peats and Putts – the back 9 will be published in 2023. The author returns to Scotland five years after publishing his first book to explore more distilleries and golf courses and finds that while much has changed, much has also reassuringly stayed the same.'

Contents

Preface

'*Expect the unexpected*' is a maxim by which I have increasingly led my life. And for golfers of all abilities it is, I contend, a maxim which will not only help improve their performances but, more importantly, increase their enjoyment of this wonderful pastime. It may show signs of desperation if I try and extend this once again to a relevant axiom by which to enjoy the imbibing of whisky too, though I think it is not without relevance. I have spoken before how every whisky in every bottle is different, and sometimes a surprise, and that it is not the drink for those who strive for certainty and uniformity.

Where am I heading with this? To Europe, which is the subject of this, my third, book on whisky and golf. As I will explain, it is a book which will encounter very little certainty and very little uniformity so if you yearn for diversity and a sense of adventure, please read on. I have also written before about the importance of context in everything and this book was written amidst the unfurling of three major historical events; first, the interminable Brexit debates within the UK which dominated the media in 2019; secondly, and more profoundly, the Covid 19 pandemic which dominated the world's agenda during 2020 and 2021; and thirdly, and more profoundly still, the horrific events in Ukraine which, just as Covid was waning, dominated our attention from early 2022. It would be foolish to ignore these given the relevance to the subject matter of Brexit and the all-consuming global impact of the Covid pandemic and the Ukranian war. Broadly I had researched half of this book in 2019 and had a plan to research the second half in 2020. That plan, as with everyone's plans for 2020, had to be seriously modified. Expect the unexpected. You get my drift.

'Europe? So are you going to look at wine and golf?' This was the most common reaction to telling friends that my next book would cover Europe. While there is an acknowledgement that golf is played across the continent, few people expect there to be whisky distilleries in Europe; North America, Japan and possibly Asia, yes, but Europe? Yet in this increasingly globalised society, whisky has become an internationally recognised product and, as it is a growing market, you would expect distilleries to emerge across the world providing the climatic conditions allow. As I pointed out in *Of Peats and Putts*, the country with the highest per capita consumption of whisky is not one of the main producing countries but in fact France. Likewise, the Scandinavians are some of the greatest connoisseurs of premium Scotch malts. Therefore, to find that there are whisky distilleries in most continental European countries was not a surprise and merited some further research.

Golf too is now a global industry. While there is interesting history in some European countries, particularly France, it was, until relatively recently, a very elitist sport, much more so than in the UK and the US. It remains today probably somewhat niche but has become more mainstream since the emergence of many European star golfers from the 1970s onwards – Seve Ballesteros from Spain and Bernhard Langer from Germany were the first superstar continental European golfers but they have since been joined by other Major winners such as José

Maria Olazabal, Sergio Garcia and Jon Rahm from Spain, Martin Kaymer from Germany, Henrik Stenson from Sweden and Francesco Molinari from Italy. Indeed, as I write, there are golfers in the World's official Men's and Women's Top 100 rankings from Spain, Italy, France, Holland, Belgium, Germany, Austria, Slovenia, Denmark, Sweden, Finland and Norway. A few years ago who would have expected a Norwegian, Victor Hovland, to win the US Amateur in 2018? He has since become one of the world's top professional golfers so golf in Europe has spread and is not just represented in isolated pockets.

Having justified my decision to choose Europe what am I planning to explore? It is true that outside of Scotland there are likely to be fewer direct associations between whisky distilleries and golf courses and I will not seek to contrive links between the two. I expect, however, many connections back to Scotland be it in the design of distilleries and courses and sometimes the people involved. I have decided to stick to my formula of nine chapters and with a degree of geographical proximity between the golf courses and distilleries, though I have had to extend the definition of 'proximate' and in a couple of instances I have, for good reason, broken the rule. The choices are not intended to facilitate a modern day European 'Grand Tour' but to explore and illustrate the development of golf and whisky in each particular country.

I have again tried to choose venues for both the golf courses and the distilleries where the local environment and landscape is worth the visit itself. I have spoken before of the importance of the local landscape to both pastimes and this remains the case in most of my choices. Again, links and seaside courses predominate as do courses and clubs with a history. The distilleries are a mixture of older established ones and new start-ups; in this case the older established ones have a history of distilling local spirit and have then more recently looked to add whisky to their portfolio as the market grows. Very often, at both the golf courses and the distilleries, there are links to Scotland or, at very least, inspiration derived from Scotland.

I will want to understand what are the different experiences of golf and whisky in Europe compared with what I learned on my visits to Scotland and subsequently England, Wales and Ireland. Clearly golf and whisky distilling are much more minority activities than they are in the United Kingdom and Ireland but this does not imply any less passion; indeed, often those involved are much more zealous as they seek to evangelise about the wonders of golf and whisky in order to educate their countrymen.

I have written before about the importance of context in enjoying and understanding both golf and whisky. For example, your memories of a course can be influenced by the weather on the day or by how well you played. Your enjoyment a dram of whisky can be heavily influenced by your mood or the company you kept when consuming it.

As to Brexit and Covid 19, just a few observations so that we can then (mostly) leave them both behind. You will be pleased to hear that on the Brexit issue I will not be commenting directly on the merits of it or otherwise save to say that, perhaps unusually, I have always seen respectable arguments on both sides of the debate. Yet, depressingly, the behaviour of many on both sides in making their respective cases has at times been less than respectable. What I do want to say is that whatever our political, constitutional or commercial relationship ends up being with our continental neighbours, I firmly believe that these relationships will continue to be strong ones. In a sense I have always felt that Brexit or no Brexit in some ways is not that important and my various interactions with likeminded citizens across Europe have only confirmed in me that view. In the long term, we will continue to seek common ground and friendships and the topics of golf and whisky provide this. While for the most part in my travels I found a degree of disappointment at the prospect of Brexit, this was by no means an exclusive position. I was particularly struck by an elderly lady in Denmark who asked me what I felt about Brexit. I had practised an embarrassed look at my feet which usually served as a signal to move onto a different subject but in this case elicited a surprise follow up: 'Well, I think it is a very good idea. I don't trust those politicians in Brussels at all. Good for you'.

Covid 19 is altogether a much more serious matter. Its relevance to this book? Well, it impacted my writing of it as the lockdown in Spain happened while I was researching my first chapter in Granada and required a hastily arranged flight back home before I could enjoy the golfing part of my Spanish trip. What the outbreak confirmed was my belief in the unpredictability of life which every round of golf symbolises. No individual, whatever their preparation, their skill, their motivation, is in control of their destiny. We can all practise 'risk management' but generally the biggest risks are those we don't recognise; the 'unknown unknowns'. How many companies in their compulsory corporate reporting of 'identifiable risks' to their businesses mentioned a global coronavirus pandemic? I remember the wise words of the Liberal politician and historian, H A L Fisher, who wrote that those studying history 'should recognise in the development of human destinies, the role of the contingent and the unforeseen.' Certainly, many a promising golf round of mine has been impacted by the unforeseen and I am sure that many start-up whisky distillers will recognise this truth.

I will not comment on war only to point out as someone who studied history for my degree, that we are always at risk from the vagaries of individual human frailties – arrogance, egotism, self-importance etc. – if we don't have political structures which can prevent these doing lasting harm. What golf does is to expose these frailties and generally prove that they lead to failure.

What both golf and whisky demonstrate is a universality in pursuing passions. Both golf and whisky are relatively niche pastimes but both attract people from a wide range of backgrounds and cultures. I found that many of the elements that have attracted me to them are recognised by Danes, Italians and Germans alike. A particular joy of writing this book has been meeting so many different characters in each of the different countries: whisky enthusiasts from Eduardo at the Liber distillery in Granada to Lena at Puni in Italy; Hans and Patrick in the Netherlands, Henrik in Sweden and Roar in Norway; and those with a passion for golf from Mikael and Niels in Denmark and Jeremy, an Irishman from Ballybunion, at Lofoten inside the Arctic Circle in Norway. I will persist with, and indeed continue to develop, my 'golf and whisky as metaphors for life' theme as the more I examine the two the more I find to support my hypothesis. The continual search for the unattainable faultless round of golf and perfect malt whisky only reminds us that life is a series of things that go well and things that go badly. Golf gives all of us moments of perfection to enjoy but also persists in reminding us that you can never bask too long in such indulgence.

Finally, I will continuously refer to that *'joy to be alive feeling'*, an expression coined by Lorne Smith in his *Fine Golf* website. I make no apologies that it is my main motivation for visiting and playing new golf courses. Golf is a sport, it is exercise, it is fun but the best golf is more than that. The same should be true of whisky; visiting distilleries and learning about whisky makes the drinking experience that much richer. The pandemic has brought into greater focus the importance of mental health and for me golf and whisky can help positively deliver that. I hope that reading the chapters that follow can contribute in some small way to your own mental well-being.

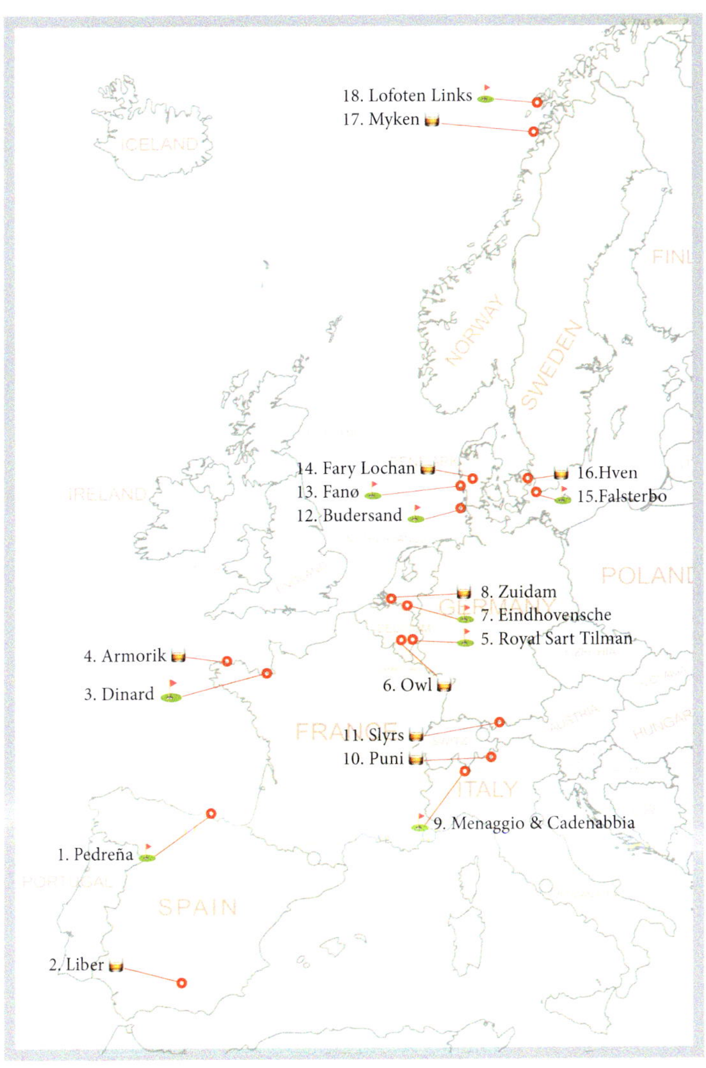

18. Lofoten Links
17. Myken
ICELAND
NORWAY
SWEDEN
14. Fary Lochan
13. Fanø
12. Budersand
16.Hven
15.Falsterbo
IRELAND
POLAND
8. Zuidam
7. Eindhovensche
5. Royal Sart Tilman
4. Armorik
3. Dinard
6. Owl
FRANCE
11. Slyrs
10. Puni
ITALY
9. Menaggio & Cadenabbia
1. Pedreña
SPAIN
2. Liber

The beautiful 14th hole at Pedreña with
Santander Bay in the background.

CHAPTER ONE

SPAIN

'Golf is the esperanto of sport'

Henry Longhurst (1909-1978)
British golf writer and commentator

On 1st January 1974, the Spanish Golf Federation awarded a professional player's card to a 16-year-old golfer from a poor family in a small town just east of Santander on the country's north coast. He became Spain's youngest ever professional golfer. That summer he won Spain's under-25 Championship on his home course at Pedrena and just two years later, having led the field after 54 holes, he finished second alongside Jack Nicklaus, to Johnny Miller in the Open Championship at Royal Birkdale. The golfer in question was, of course, Severiano Ballesteros or 'Seve' as he became known the world over. It is not an exaggeration to say that it was Seve more than anyone else who was responsible for igniting the widespread interest in golf, not just in Spain but across Europe, which led to the enormous growth of the European Tour over the next three decades.

It therefore seems only right to start by examining the development of golf in Europe, not only in Spain but at Pedrena. In 1970 there were just 35 courses in Spain and an estimated 15,000 golfers. Today there are nearly 400 courses and 350,000 players. And Spain has become a popular destination for British holiday golfers particularly to courses on the Mediterranean coast most of which were built as a result of the upsurge in interest in golf prompted by Seve's extraordinary career.

As there are only two whisky distilleries in Spain, I have had to compromise on my old rule of geographical proximity. The biggest and oldest is near Segovia in the centre of Spain where there are a few courses of interest, particularly near the capital Madrid. The newer one is near Granada where there is little in terms of golfing excellence. Therefore, this Spanish chapter will be a two-centre trip conveniently facilitated by the existence of an internal flight from Bilbao to Granada.

I will start in Granada as it is the southernmost point of this tour and I will end in Chapter 9 at the most northerly point, some 3,000 miles away. Granada is one of the most southerly points of all Europe and therefore perhaps an unlikely venue for whisky distilling. Its population of about 230,000 makes it a similar size to Aberdeen in Scotland but it is a popular tourist destination because of the famous Alhambra which towers over the city. The rest of the city is quite compact with an old area around the cathedral and some medieval streets up in the Albaicin area. The Alhambra is impressive for its history dating back to the Moorish era, its imposing palaces and buildings and extensive gardens. From its elevated position, it not only looks out over the city below but there are magnificent views of the entire valley surrounded by the snow-capped Sierra Nevada mountains. If you follow the valley southwards, the first town of any significant size you come to is Padul where the first malt whisky to be produced in Spain originated. Padul used to be called El Padul and recently the inhabitants have started to restore the definite article to the official name. The town is unexceptional but has a number of interesting historical buildings and its setting at the foothills of the Sierra Nevada is attractive.

The more immediate environment of the distillery is less inviting, being on a small industrial estate at the northern end of the town. The building itself is simply an industrial shed though it has a local, Moorish-style façade, a small but welcome architectural feature.

A cask at Liber from 2008 filled during a Roger Waters concert in Granada

This is perhaps the first distillery that I have featured which is not open to the public. Here there are no formal tours; there is no 'visitor centre'. It is a small private business which is finding its way and is artisanal in many respects. The business is run by Fran Peregrina who is very welcoming but speaks very little English – indeed about as much as I speak Spanish, which amounts to not much more than the ability to order a paella and a bottle of rioja. Fortunately for my visit, after being welcomed by Fran, I am shown around by Eduardo whose command of English is excellent and who also has a strong passion for the distillery and its product.

Somewhat surprisingly, Liber does not really belong to the series of start-ups that have flourished since the whisky revival of the last ten years as it opened as far back as 2001. It is unashamedly artisanal in feel with the whole process undertaken on the small site, including underground storage of the maturing spirit. There is an old mill for grinding the barley, a mash tun and washbacks plus two copper stills which are, and look, handmade. They are somewhat eccentrically shaped with cylindrical bases and narrow onion-like tops and they have a distinctively 'Moorish' look to them. The product is chill-filtered, rather against the current trend, and bottled on site.

Perhaps the best part of the informal tour – there was no distilling happening on the Friday I visited – is the maturation warehouse. To reach it, you have to clamber rather precariously down a steep ramp into the underground cellar. It is understandable that the maturing spirit is kept here as the summer temperatures regularly reach into the 30s. This clearly affects the rate of maturation as does the wide temperature range – in winter it can also fall almost to zero. We will see this issue also in other European countries. The default wood used is American oak but they also obviously use Spanish sherry butts. What is most distinctive is that each barrel is marked on the front in chalk with not only the year of its filling but also the celebration of an event – the one which Eduardo was most keen to show off was a concert held in Granada in 2008 by Roger Waters of Pink Floyd. Whether this will become a Pink Floyd bottling I am not sure. Another cask commemorated Spain's World Cup victory in 2010.

Marketing seems to be an issue. This business has been around for some 20 years but the brand is hardly established and very little is exported. Indeed, it seems that the business is sustained by the manufacture of other spirits – rum, gin, vodka and liqueurs, mainly for third parties. While many of the start-ups across Scotland, Ireland and indeed other European countries (most of which dated from after 2010) are successfully commanding a premium for their niche brands, Liber has struggled to do this. I think that there are perhaps two reasons. First, they were ahead of the trend, maybe too early into the market which really took off after the global financial crisis in 2008; it is not always an advantage to be a pioneer. Secondly, I sense that the Spanish market for whisky is different and strongly influenced by the other distillery in Spain, Distilerio Molino del Arco, which is famous for producing its cheap blended Whisky DYC. This has dominated the Spanish market and seems to have squeezed out the malts. It is noteworthy that Spain appears in sixth place in the table of consumption of Blended Scotch but not at all in the top ten countries for consumption of Malt Scotch. Germany and Italy for example are strong consumers of Single Malt Scotch but not of blends. (The French, of course, are heavy consumers of both.) Whisky DYC, now owned by Beam Suntory, has started producing a malt whisky though this is a 'Pure Malt' blend from some of Beam Suntory's Scottish distilleries. I have been amazed at how the many small start-up distilleries have created ways of adding value: selling casks up front, visitor centres, yearly bottlings of different expressions, all communicated via a strong presence on social media. This has to be the way forward for Liber. Their product is good and, being the only Spanish-produced malt whisky, it is distinctive, but they need to ignore the current Spanish-market price-conventions and charge much higher prices and look to gain an export presence. I sense that there is considerable value held in their stock if they can realise it. Maybe the answer lies in those chalk commemorations on the barrels – I think a bottling of Spanish World Cup Victory 2010 Malt Whisky would command a good premium. The product definitely deserves more widespread recognition.

That afternoon, I decided to explore the Sierra Nevada mountains. The landscape in southern Spain is on a different scale to Scotland and Ireland. Mulhacen, the highest peak in the Sierra Nevada is over 11,000 feet, over two-and-a-half times the height of Ben Nevis. I headed for Capiliera, the highest of a number of pretty villages (it is also higher than Ben Nevis) offering spectacular views down the mountain gorge. The road up is a little scary at times (though wait until you read the Italian chapter; this was, by comparison, a breeze) but definitely worth the trip. The village is a centre for walking and offers a good selection of unfussy restaurants.

As I sat outside in the square in Capiliera, eating some local ham and enjoying the views, all seemed well with the world. Or perhaps I was a bit naïve. The plan was to visit the Alhambra over the weekend, before flying up to Bilbao from where, as well as visiting Pedrena, I would take the opportunity of seeing the Guggenheim Museum.

That evening, the centre of Granada was lively though not overly busy. All the restaurants were open but perhaps there was a sense that something was not right. It was the following day that the Spanish Prime Minister addressed the nation and announced an immediate lockdown. The hotel from near Bilbao got in touch to say that they were closing; the visit to Pedrena would have to wait. The immediate concern was how to get home. Being the only person in my hotel in the centre of Granada overlooking a deserted Alhambra, one of the country's busiest tourist attractions, was a strange experience, especially as the only food available was from a local supermarket. Still, the flight to Bilbao went ahead and I was able to take an immediate flight home to the UK.

It was two years before I could return.

The impact of Seve on the rise of European golf cannot be overplayed. It was not just that he was a great golfer; he was also a great personality. It was not only the quality of his golf that attracted but the style of his golf, a style that for many transformed the image of the game. Seve probably played more bad shots than any other great golfer but he also played, by necessity, more miraculously good ones. Indeed, he became famous for many of these miracle shots: the deft pitch over the bunker on the 18th at Royal Birkdale to secure a share of second place in his first Open Championship; the famous 3-wood hit out of a bunker (yes, a 3-wood out of a bunker) in the Ryder Cup in Florida in 1981; or, perhaps most memorable of all, the wedge from an impossible position, through a tiny gap in the trees, over a seven-foot-high wall to the final green at Crans Montana in Switzerland in 1993. This 'impossible shot' ended up behind a bunker just short of the green from where with the same club he inevitably holed the pitch for a winning birdie three.

Being brought up in Scotland, I was already interested in golf when Seve emerged but he did become my golfing hero. He certainly gave me my favourite live spectator moment in any sport. 'I was there', as they say, on that famous occasion when he sunk that putt on the 18th green at St. Andrews to win the 1984 Open Championship, making the celebratory punches of the air which were to become iconic. I was actually watching Tom Watson having his misfortunes on the road at 17 but had a clear view up the 18th fairway, heard the enormous cheer when the ball, which hovered momentarily on the lip before dropping in the hole (some say it was Seve's iron will rather than gravity which caused it to drop) and then witnessed the famous celebration from afar. A moment never to be forgotten.

Ballesteros burst on the golfing scene in the mid-1970s and became an immediate star. He was young, handsome, enigmatic and played with a flair which attracted a new audience to what was still at the time regarded as something of a stuffy old game played mainly by the middle classes and Americans. Yes, there were some good players in the UK and Europe but none were household names, though Tony Jacklin's victory in the US Open in 1970 had started to broaden the game's appeal this side of the Atlantic. But Seve was something different. I talked in my last book about the concept of the flawed genius and Seve was the epitome of this; one of his biographies, by Robert Green, has '*Golf's Flawed Genius*' as its subtitle. In some ways it was Seve's flaws as much as his genius which appealed to such a wide audience and, in this respect, Seve symbolises golf as life. Just as his rise to fame was meteoric, so too was the decline in his game after his final Major victory at Royal Lytham St. Anne's in 1988. Few realised the extent of the back injury from which he had suffered since he was a teenager and perhaps the increasing unreliability of his game through the 1990s was a result of the early effects of a then undiagnosed illness. His premature death at the age of just 56 from a brain tumour is a poignant reminder of life's uncertainties.

Pedrena is an unremarkable town on the eastern bank of Santander Bay with views over to the city on the other side. There are ferries to Santander from southern England and a small airport (aptly named the Aeropuerto de Seve Ballesteros) but I flew into Bilbao about an hour's drive away to the east. Bilbao is perhaps a more interesting city with the spectacular Guggenheim Museum definitely the highlight. I also happened upon a tapas bar in the Plaza Nueva in the old town which had quite an extensive whisky collection including a 1968 Macallan. Unfortunately, my Spanish was not good enough to enquire about its provenance.

Surprisingly, the golf course lies on the inland side of the town, high up on a peninsula with one side overlooking the bay and the other two sides overlooking the substantial estuary of the river Cubas. Real Golf de Pedrena is a relatively old course for Spain which opened in 1928 and had quite a prestigious membership; the first Honorary President was the last King of Spain, Alphonso VIII and the President was the Duke of Alba. They clearly had both influence and money as they commissioned none other than Harry Colt to design the layout. As you approach the club up the substantial driveway there is an 'old money' feel about the place. It is very different from the modern resort courses on the Mediterranean coast. While visitors are welcomed there is no marketing effort to attract them and members are very much prioritised. I was asked to ring up the day before to confirm that

I was coming and they would then find a suitable time for me to play.

The wisteria-clad clubhouse has a 'country club' feel to it and facilities include a pool, children's club and padel court. There is an impressive practice range and I hired clubs from the biggest golf-club store I have ever seen – it was almost as big as the clubhouse. Clearly members here don't take their clubs home, something more common in Europe. The car park was quite busy when I arrived mid-morning though there didn't seem to be many golfers. It transpired that a number of ladies four-balls (I was to see them on the course later – they were all dressed in red tartan which looked very smart) had gone off earlier and there were a number of male groups going off in the afternoon but there was plenty of time in between. I went off on my own at midday and noticed a number of other singletons followed me later on. They were too far behind me to suggest joining up and I am always conscious that often players are playing on their own because they want to. I often do this; if I want to practice, I much prefer playing a few holes on my own than spending time on a practice range where I generally get bored after about ten minutes. There is a pitch and putt course and a new 9-hole course designed by Seve, squeezed in on land between the main course and the town and estuary. I didn't play it but it looked much tighter than the main course and with smaller greens. I think it would require what you could call 'shot-making', something I'm all in favour of.

It was a pleasant warm day in late March. I've already mentioned the wisteria on the clubhouse – at least a month earlier than I am used to in England – but as well as other mature shrubs around the clubhouse there were flashes of azalea around the course which added to the attraction of the surroundings. The course is quite hilly though never over-steep. Most holes have changes of elevation which Colt has used to good effect in the layout. As ever, changes had been made over the years to the course, not always positive ones, and it is worth noting that the most recent work being undertaken by David Williams has the brief both to modernise as well as recover some of the Colt design identity. For example, work in the 1970s had lengthened holes 9 and 11 to Par 5s but in doing so had completely changed the Par 3 10th which many had regarded as a classic Colt Par 3. This has now been largely restored. When I visited there was a lot of work being undertaken with the second hole, also a Par 3, being completely renovated. The Par 3s, as with many Colt courses, are certainly some of the highlights. Four of the five use elevation change in one way or another and all 'look' good. The second looked as if it will be a classic: a long carry up a gentle slope with water to the right (though only catching a bad miss). The 7th plays downhill across a valley to an offset green. I can see why the 10th was restored to its original glory; again, it plays across a valley to a narrow but long green with cavernous bunkers right and an awkward bank to the left. The 12th is perhaps the least interesting (though I nearly holed my bunker shot for what would have been an unlikely two) while the final Par 3, 15, plays over 200 yards but is sharply downhill and with the prevailing wind behind will be usually quite accessible. Just don't miss it right!

Perhaps a few more holes should be mentioned; the 8th is a very sharp dogleg to the right and then uphill to a green perched above the estuary. Do not think about cutting the corner or, if you have not fallen off the high cliff down to the estuary, you will at best have to play an extremely awkward shot from rough. The 14th is perhaps the best-known hole: a drive up to the top of a hill from where you have a relatively short downhill second to a green sitting framed against the backdrop of Santander Bay – a very pretty hole. 16 is a rollercoaster Par 5 and 17 another strong dog-leg, this time sharply downhill from an elevated tee where, again, you need to keep left to have a decent view of the green. There is perhaps more variety and interest on the back 9 but there isn't a weak hole. And the turf, while not 'links', is sandy and springy, ideal for golf.

And, importantly, the environment is engaging: mature attractive parkland with a range of views offered up at various parts of the course whether from elevated tees across the course, in towards the estuary or out over Santander Bay. I used the word 'environment' rather than 'ambience', because on the day I visited I can't describe the setting as peaceful. The reason for this was the amount of work being done on the course. This is not a complaint; it was late March which is a good time for greenkeepers to be working on getting a course up to its best for the late spring and summer peak season. I have already mentioned the substantial works being undertaken on the 2nd hole. But that was only part of it. John Deere was everywhere: tractors and trailers, diggers and strimmers, mowers and blowers, you name it, every bit of kit imaginable. I actually noticed one red Toro tractor which looked a bit out-of-place amidst the predominant green of John Deere. I was simply amazed at the number of people working on the course – it probably explained why the car park was so full. They were all respectful and would turn off whatever contraption they were operating when I was playing a shot so had been well briefed. It suggests that the club is in good health.

The inside of the clubhouse is spacious and airy and traditional in style. There are large dining rooms which were set with the full silver service so geared up for proper dining, including the Seve Ballesteros Salon which contained many of the classic pictures of him as well as a record of his considerable achievements. For me, visiting Pedrena was something of a pilgrimage and I am slightly surprised more people don't do it. The club is clearly proud of Seve but nothing is overdone. You can somehow feel his presence and imagine how, after practicing on the beach, he would wait until dusk to climb over the fence and play a few holes. And presence was what Seve had – the force of his personality drove many of his achievements and, in particular, how he more than anyone transformed the Ryder Cup from a one-sided affair to an event which Europe began to dominate. In the 25 years from 1985, Europe's first victory since 1957, Europe won 8 times, the USA 4 times with one drawn match. Many also attribute the extraordinary comeback victory by Europe at Medinah in 2011, a year after Seve's death, to his presence beyond the grave. Such was the legend of Seve.

The dramatic Art Deco clubhouse at Dinard

The trees on Dinard hint at the prevailing wind direction

CHAPTER TWO

FRANCE

'I would like to see the fairways more narrow. Then everyone would have to play from the rough, not just me'

Severiano Ballesteros (1957-2011)

Spanish professional golfer; winner of five major championships

FRANCE IS AN enigma. Like many British people, I have a strong affinity for the country, its people, its traditions and its culture. Yet, also like many, I feel a sense of rivalry and politically over the years there have been tensions, the Brexit debate being simply the latest manifestation. Friendship and rivalry are often not far apart. However, as demonstrated by France's sympathetic reaction to the death of Queen Elizabeth, so warmly expressed in the eloquent tribute from President Macron, there is so much more that unites us than divides us. So too with whisky and golf.

Golf is a minority sport within France yet the country boasts a fine golfing tradition and there are many great courses, with four in the current Top 10 in Europe. In particular, the surrounds of Paris are home to the likes of Morfontaine, Chantilly and Fontainebleu, top-class heathland-style courses which are a match for the best that Surrey can offer in England. Most of these are the work of an architect who is less well known than the likes of Harry Colt, James Braid and Alister Mackenzie but who in Europe has perhaps a bigger and better portfolio than any of those greats – Tom Simpson. I was tempted to visit this area though some of these courses, like Morfontaine, require you to play with a member. Perhaps the one with the best history is in fact the La Vallée course at La Boulie, designed by Willie Park Junior and owned by the Racing Club de France. The first French Open was held here in 1906 and won by Arnaud Massey who, the following year at Hoylake, became the first international player to win The Open – indeed he remains today the only Frenchman to have ever won The Open. La Boulie had held more French Opens than any other course until quite recently when it was overtaken by Le Golf National which has become the regular venue since it first held the tournament in 1991. Winners of the French Open at La Boulie make an impressive list including J H Taylor, Braid, Hagan, Faldo and Ballesteros, who won the last tournament to be held there in 1986. It is a fine course and has a delightful clubhouse and restaurant.

Another area of France which deserves a mention is the far south-west. There you have the oldest course in continental Europe at Pau which dates back to 1856 though there is evidence of golf being played there by two Scottish officers in Wellington's army in 1814. The course is set attractively near the centre of the town on the banks of the Gave river and while it won't appear in a list of France's top courses it is a pleasant location and the history gives it a special feeling. The better-known courses in the area are about an hour-and-a-half away on the coast where there are some impressive modern layouts at the likes of Seignoisse, Medoc and Moliets. From a historical point of view, Biarritz Le Phare and Chiberta are perhaps more interesting, Willie Dunn and Colt designing the former and Tom Simpson the latter. Arnaud Massey was born in Biarritz and there is a fine statue of him outside the smart clubhouse at Le Phare. He also later became the professional at the other famous course in this area, Chantaco, which was designed by Harry Colt and opened in 1928.

The far north-east also boasts a small clutch of great and attractive courses – three are rated in France's Top 10. The new kid on the block – it opened in 2010 – is Belle Dune which is very well-regarded and set in the stunningly beautiful Marquenterre reserve. The most northerly is Wimereux which is a links course dating back to 1901, while the most famous are probably Le Touquet and Hardelot which have been popular with British golf tourists for their accessibility. Both these clubs have two courses: La Mer and Le Foret at the former and Les Pins and Les Dunes at the latter. Colt and Alison designed La Mer at Le Touquet and Tom Simpson Les Pins at Hardelot and this latter one is usually the highest rated. Hardelot is a pleasant resort on the Opal Coast – named so as the light reflecting off the chalk cliffs above the long sandy beaches resembles that of the stone. It attracted painters such as Monet and Manet as well as Turner and was much favoured by the British in Edwardian times. The course is slightly inland so not a true links but it offers a number of memorable holes: the five Par 3s all use elevation changes to good effect, there are a couple of interesting short Par 4s while perhaps the most distinctive hole is the 15th, a strategic conundrum which gives you the choice of driving either side of a small copse in the middle of the fairway; there's more room to the left than the right but the uphill second will be longer and from a tricky angle. We will experience more of Tom Simpson's designs in the next chapter.

What about France and whisky? One of the most surprising facts I learnt while writing my first book on whisky was that France has the highest per capita consumption of Scotch in the world. This is largely Blended Scotch with a number of brands marketed specifically for the French market. France is also a big market for Single Malt Scotch though it lags the US in volume. It would seem natural therefore that a home-grown whisky industry would develop and indeed this is the case with currently up to fifty distilleries making whisky in France. The majority, however, are distilleries which have added whisky to their portfolios as the market has developed; many are old fruit liqueur or genever distilleries. Genever is a sort of hybrid between gin and whisky, an unaged malted spirit which is often blended with a neutral grain spirit, and is popular particularly in the Benelux countries.

The first French whisky did not appear on the market until 1998, but the taste for French-produced whisky is increasing. In 2010 only 210,000 bottles of French whisky were consumed in France but this had grown to over a million by 2018 and is estimated to reach five million by 2025. There were only a handful of distilleries at the turn of the century but there are now over eighty. The greatest concentration of these is in the east where there are few golf courses of note. Neither Paris nor the south-west, which provide good options on golf locations, have distilleries to visit. I have decided therefore to go to Brittany where we find France's oldest whisky distillery at Lannion and, conveniently, its second oldest golf course at Dinard. It is worth noting that France's second oldest golf course pre-dates the oldest malt whisky distillery by some 100 years.

From the UK, the quickest route to Brittany is by ferry; you can travel either from Plymouth to Roscoff in the west or from Portsmouth to St. Malo further to the east. I did the latter and I can highly recommend St. Malo as a place to stay with its old town walls, many harbours and beaches, hotels and vibrant restaurants. It is very French in a comforting, traditional way. Dinard is only a few miles away over the other side of the broad Rance estuary. Dinard has a slightly different atmosphere, more monied, with grand villas and was a popular resort during *La Belle Epoque.* While the golf course dates from this time, 1887, it is not actually in Dinard but a few miles further along the coast in Saint-Briac-sur- Mer, one of a number of small, smart villages along what is called the Emerald Coast. The club was founded in the 1880s by British servicemen who commissioned the North Berwick born architect, Tom Dunn, to lay out a course on a piece of heathland overlooking the coast occupied at the time by gorse, broom and cattle. It soon became one of France's most prestigious clubs, hosting many early tournaments.

Tom Dunn was part of a famous Scottish golfing family. Tom's father was Tom Dunn Snr. from Musselburgh who spent time as the greenkeeper at Blackheath before returning to Scotland. Tom was his eldest son and he started his career at North Berwick then moved to Wimbledon where he extended the original course on the Common to 18 holes – a course which at the time was shared by Royal Wimbledon and the London Scottish Club. His other famous designs were Royal Worlington and Lindrick. His younger brother, Willie

Jnr, became a successful professional, coming runner-up in the first ever US Open in 1895. He worked at Westward Ho! where he redesigned the course and in America was involved in adding holes to the original Shinnecock Hills. He also had connections in France, spending many years at Biarritz. Tom married Isabella Gourlay from another famous Scottish golfing family and their progeny, three sons and a daughter, were all involved with golf. Perhaps the most famous was Isabella May Gourlay Dunn, known as 'Queenie', who became America's first ever female professional golfer. It does not stop there as Tom's sister married Will Tucker who became a renowned golfer, club maker and architect in America. A whole book could be written on the Dunn family.

It's worth also discussing the great figures of French golf. For today's audience it is perhaps a story of many good golfers who have not quite made it to the very top of the game. Jean van de Velde became famous for all the wrong reasons while the likes of Victor Dubuisson and Thomas Levet have never quite fulfilled their promise. Perhaps France's latest young star, Victor Perez, will buck this trend. No French player has played in more than one Ryder Cup though France has had much greater representation in the Solheim Cup. However, going back in history, France has produced some greats, especially in the women's game. Three amateur golfers in particular deserve a mention: Lally Segard, Simone Thion de la Chaume and her daughter Catherine Lacoste.

Lally Segard became one of the first Honorary lady members of the R&A. In her career she won over thirty national titles including the British Ladies Open Amateur Championship in 1950. She became known as 'la vicomtesse' following her marriage in 1939 to Vicomte Jacques de Saint-Saveur. Latterly she became an influential promoter and organiser of Ladies golf. Simone Thion de la Chaume was the greatest French player of the 1920s, winning the British Ladies Amateur in 1927. She married the French tennis star René Lacoste who won seven tennis major championships including both Wimbledon and the US Open twice. Their daughter was Catherine Lacoste who was to become one of the best lady golfers of the 1960s, winning, as well as the US and British Ladies Amateur Championships, the US Ladies Open in 1967, the only amateur to have achieved this. She could easily have become a professional but retired from competitive golf in her mid-twenties.

The layout at Dinard has changed over the years and it is not totally clear which holes are Tom Dunn's original work. The course is divided into two with the opening 7 holes being played on land to the east with the remaining 11 along the coast in front of the west-facing clubhouse. Let us start with the clubhouse as it is by some way Dinard's most distinctive feature, a classic and imposing three-floor art-deco structure sitting high above the course. I say 'imposing' though from the roadside and car park it is less so but from the practice ground and 18th green you get the best view of its grandeur. The top floor comprises a reception area and then a charming open-plan bar and dining lounge with a balcony which looks out over the course. Downstairs are locker rooms and club storage. It was built in 1927, replacing the original wooden building (from 1887) and was designed by a specialist art deco architect, Marcel Oudin. It has recently been listed as an historic monument. At the same time as its listing, it was refurbished under the supervision of the heritage authorities. Apart from its architectural merit, what I liked about it was the atmosphere; it was a hive of activity with golfers drinking and eating and enjoying themselves. This is a proper local golf club, seemingly quite diverse in its membership, and not at all exclusive. In that respect it resembles many old Scottish clubs. I had booked to tee off at 3pm and was paired with a local member, Christian, his wife and a younger friend who had only taken up golf two months previously. Magnus, the younger friend, started impressively given his novice status though understandably began to struggle later on in the round. Christian and his wife Agnes were both very steady, the former also managing to hole at least four long putts. His English was probably even less fluent than my French but when I told him on the 18th green, after he had holed yet another 15-footer, how good a putter he was, he merely shrugged and said 'Aujourd'hui, Oui, mais…!' Such is golf.

The first five holes are nothing special. After a good opener which plays straight uphill along a very bumpy fairway you cross the road for four holes. They are not uninteresting but nothing particularly memorable. You then cross back over the road – quite a long walk – and play two holes on the seaward side of the 1st. The 6th, a short Par 4 squeezed alongside the coastal path, is a great hole, only some 330 yards but very much typical of the best that Dinard offers. You play down from a high tee to a dramatically undulating fairway with a bunker in the middle before the hole rises sharply to a green nestling on the top of the cliff. I played a 3 wood (a driver would have brought the bunker into play) towards the safety of the left-hand side of the fairway and was pleased with my shot. However, somehow it ended up just holding onto the right-hand side! Certainly, some local knowledge is required to know where to land it. 7 is the first of the Par 3s, a solid test, before you walk past the clubhouse and the Pro-Shop to play the final 11 holes. These final 11 holes, being shorter and tightly packed with no long walks in between, will take you about the same time to play as the first 7. The best section of the course is from 10-16. 11 and 12 are both worth a mention; the first being similar to the 7th, requiring a careful tee shot to a fairway that slopes dramatically to the sea before an uphill, slightly blind second to the green; and the 12th, a short Par 3 with a deceptive green which you simply mustn't miss right. I should have spotted this when Christian played his shot, what looked to be a long way left but wasn't. Fortunately, my slightly right-of-centre shot somehow just clung on precariously to the right-hand edge of the green. 14 is also a good Par 4, requiring a solid second to carry a series of bunkers and a ridge which the green sits above. 16 is a Par 4 with a sharp left to right dog-leg. I was happy with my tee shot which seemed to be in the middle of the fairway only to find when I got there that there was a tree directly in line with the pin – rather like the 5th at Huntercombe. I impressed my playing partners by playing a long sweeping fade around it which found the green – very satisfying. 17 is an extremely short downhill Par 3 called, appropriately, 'Le Juge', and 18 is a finishing version of the first hole, requiring two solid strokes to reach the green which sits below the clubhouse.

This is by no means a great golf course. It is neither in design terms nor scale in the same league as Hardelot, but it is great fun to play and the sea views are tremendous. It has, particularly on the back 9, the feel of Sheringham, a sort of gentle cliff-top links, not long but always requiring accuracy and a range of shots. My playing companions were amused to see me playing into most holes along the ground, either with my putter or a rescue club but this was usually the best approach.

I have to mention, however, that the course condition was very poor. Indeed, this was also the case at both Hardelot and Wimereux which I had played a few weeks previously. In mitigation, we had experienced one of the hottest and driest summers on record but in each case the fairways were in a dreadful state and preferred lies were essential. This was one of the reasons for taking a putter or a rescue club as the risk of the turf disintegrating on even a well struck pitch shot was high. Unlike Hardelot, Dinard had no fairway watering. However, at Hardelot it was incomplete which led to patches of the fairway being very lush (far too lush in my view) and other parts being bare. It was a lottery depending on where you landed.

Fairway watering is one of those controversial issues in golf clubs, like prioritising four-balls or foursomes and whether long socks should be worn with short trousers! There are likely to be strong opinions within the membership on both sides of the argument. Some will say that if a course has survived for 100 years without fairway watering, why should vast sums of money be spent on it as it will change the nature of the course. Others will point to the challenge of maintaining the quality of fairways in a hot summer particularly with climate change likely to exacerbate the problem. My position is that fairway watering can't be a bad thing as long as it is not over-used – indeed it should only be used when necessary. Courses should get dry and bouncy in the summer and watering for the sake of it will only change the challenge. Water should be used if there is a risk of the fairways being badly damaged by weather conditions; water should be a tool to keep the fairways as they were intended. Of course, it is not only about water but about the grasses used – grasses which can withstand dry conditions are much preferable to those which can't. From an environmental perspective golf courses should be looking to minimise both water and fertiliser use and this seems to be increasingly understood.

Brittany is perhaps better known for cider than for whisky but nowadays there are a number of whisky distilleries. On the south coast, Distillerie des Menhirs has developed the Eddu whisky brand using local buckwheat – as used in Breton galettes – and Glann ar Mor at Pleubian uses quite a traditional process with a long fermentation in wooden washbacks and direct fire distillation to produce both peated and unpeated 'Celtic' whiskies. The distillery was bought in 2020 by a French spirits producer. I decided, however, to explore the oldest, Distillerie Warengheim at Lannion, less than 100 miles west along the coast from Dinard. The business was founded in 1900 by Léon Warengheim and enjoyed early success by producing a plant liqueur called Elixir d'Armorique which gained an international reputation. After the Great War, his son, Henri, took over the business and developed the product range into other fruit and herb liqueurs. During the 1960s the family joined up with Yves Leizour and the business grew as it diversified its product range and started to sell to supermarkets, necessitating a move the present site on the outskirts of the town. Yves' son Gilles, acquired the business in 1981 and it was a couple of years later that they distilled their first Breton whisky, a blend which was first sold in 1987. Its success then prompted investment in a dedicated malt whisky distillery with copper pot stills in 1993 and the first product, France's first ever single malt, was launched in 1998 under the 'Armorik' brand.

Ever since Gilles Leizour took over the company (it is now run by his son-in-law), the strategy has been to focus on regional Bretagne products with Fine de Bretagne (a cider brandy) and Pommeau de Bretagne (a blend of apple juice and cider brandy) also becoming core to their range. Other products include

A dram of Armorik – Breton whisky

include 'Chouchenn', a kind of Breton mead made with honey, as well as an artisan gin and a range of beers. From the start their whisky has been marketed not as 'French' but as 'Breton' and in 2015 they were instrumental in setting up a 'Breton Whisky' geographical indication with strict regulations as to how the product needs to be made – in the same way as the

Scotch Whisky Regulations protect the integrity of Scotch. There is now a Fédération du Whisky du Bretagne with six members. It is perhaps not surprising that a French whisky business should push the concept of '*terroir*', something taken for granted in the wine industry but which has never quite been accepted in whisky.

The approach to whisky making is fairly traditional. The distillery is sited beside a natural spring from where they get their water. They claim that this has a 'very low limestone content' given the predominance of granite in the area, though as I have said before, it is a moot point what effect this has during mashing and fermentation. The barley is organic and from Brittany though malted in Belgium given the absence of maltsters in the area. The mash tun and washbacks are stainless steel and the stills are copper, specifically designed and manufactured in Cognac. Ageing, blending and bottling, with water from the spring used for dilution, are all done on site.

As most new whisky businesses have discovered, probably the biggest impact on quality comes from the ageing and they see the local ageing in what they call 'the unique maritime climate' of Brittany as a core part of their proposition. To add to the Breton '*terroir*' angle, they have now set up a long-term partnership with the last remaining cooper in Brittany to use casks from oak grown in the far west of the region. The core range of the Armorik (*Armor* is Breton for sea) whisky brand, includes the 'Classic', matured in ex-bourbon casks, a sherry cask version, a peated edition using peated barley from Scotland, and a 'Double Maturation' which is matured initially in virgin Breton oak and then finished in sherry butts. This product has won a number of awards.

I found both Dinard, with its unstuffy community atmosphere and traditional style of course, and Armorik, with its proud local Breton twist to traditional whisky distilling, very reflective of what I like best from Scottish golf clubs and whisky distilleries.

The elegant surroundings of the first tee at Royal Sart-Tilman

The stills at the Owl Distillery transported from Caperdonich on Speyside now sit in old farm buildings with a beautiful barn ceiling

CHAPTER THREE

BELGIUM

'The element of luck, as it presents itself on our famous courses, is an essential attribute of the game at its best.'

Tom Simpson (1877-1964)

Golf course architect

Belgium has in recent years produced a number of very good young golfers with two, Nicolas Colsearts and Thomas Pieters, becoming Ryder Cup players. Perhaps, however, Belgium's greatest golfer was Flory van Donck whose record makes him the most successful continental European golfer between Arnaud Massey in the 1920s and Severiano Ballesteros in the 1970s. While van Donck never won The Open (he was twice runner-up, to Peter Thomson in 1956 and Gary Player in 1959) his record in other European Opens is remarkable. He won the Belgium and Dutch Opens five times, the Italian Open four times, the French three times, the German and Swiss twice and the Portuguese once. He was a popular player, an excellent putter and renowned for his courteous manner.

Belgium is perhaps less well known for its whisky though the Belgians are renowned for enjoying good food and drink. The Belgian tipple of preference is probably beer and indeed many of the current distillers of whisky in the country are beer brewers.

I will however, feature the one focused whisky distiller which started in 1997, a number of years before the boom in whisky distillery start-ups across the UK and Europe.

For a small country, there is a high-quality choice of golf courses to play, with British designers predominating, especially Simpson, Colt and Fred Hawtree. I have chosen an inland Simpson course as it is handily situated close to my chosen distillery in the pretty southern part of Belgium. The Belgian Owl Distillery was one of the earlier pioneers in malt whisky production in Europe, first distilling in 2004. It is situated just north of Liège where, some 20 minutes away, there is a well-regarded Tom Simpson Golf Course at Royal Sart-Tilman.

Tom Simpson was undoubtedly a very interesting character. He came from a wealthy Lancastrian mining family, like Colt studied at Cambridge University and then became a barrister. As did Colt, he gave up his legal practice to become a golf-course designer, joining Herbert Fowler's firm in 1910. He was given responsibility for its business in Europe which is why much of his finest work can be found there. Later in his career he worked with Philip Mackenzie Ross and Molly Gourlay, one of the few female golf designers at that time.

By all accounts he was a difficult person with strong opinions to accompany his considerable artistic flair. He was well known for promoting 'strategic design' and was a strong advocate for not trying to design out luck from the game. His portfolio of courses, which he either designed or worked on remodelling, reflect this creative flair: Morfontaine (usually ranked the best in continental Europe), Cruden Bay in Scotland, Ballybunion in Ireland and distinctive layouts in England such as Ashridge, The New Zealand Club, Hayling and Liphook. He was an eclectic figure with many talents, being an accomplished artist, providing illustrations for many of Bernard Darwin's famous golf columns in *Country Life*, and was a prolific writer and was also, apparently, proficientat needlework. He was well connected, designing a number of 'private courses' for the likes of Lord Mountbatten and the Rothschilds, liked expensive cars (his silver Rolls Royce was very much a trademark of his) and collected a range of items such as Persian rugs. Being opinionated with a rather abrupt and outwardly arrogant manner, he was a controversial figure but increasingly he has been recognised as one of the great golf course architects of his age.

Three of the top four courses in Belgium are his work: Royal Antwerp, Royal Belgium (Ravenstein) and Royal Sart-Tilman. (There are a lot of 'Royal' courses in Belgium as the royal family there have always been interested in golf with King Badouin even representing his country in international amateur matches.) Royal Antwerp is the highest rated and is an impressive layout with a wonderful clubhouse in an attractive wooded Antwerp suburb. It is fairly flat so perhaps lacks a little drama but the course is being constantly improved with tree removal allowing the course to get back to how it was originally intended. I also played another Tom Simpson design, Royal Fagnes, at Spa south of Liège in the Belgium Ardennes. It is in a lovely, quiet setting and enjoyable to play but I don't think Tom Simpson would recognise it. There are some wonderful holes but the club needs to employ a lumberjack or two in order to return the course to how it must originally have been. I played in October and the quality of the turf was disappointing. As the Surrey heathland courses have discovered, removing trees has enormous benefits, both in improving the look of many holes but also the quality of the turf.

Royal Sart-Tilman is a class above Fagnes. Liège is a historical city on the River Meuse which became an important industrial centre, particularly for coal mining and iron and steel making. These industries have gone into decline and some of the old works form a rather ghostly presence along the banks of the river on the outskirts of the city. The club is situated in a heavily wooded area on the southern edge of the city on land owned by the neighbouring University of Liège. It is not as old as many Simpson courses, opening in 1939 only to be occupied by the German army during the war who dug up some holes for potato growing. The course was then restored in 1947. Here the trees are more natural as Simpson basically cut through the forest to create the course – it was not an original heathland that has since been invaded by trees. The fairways are relatively wide so they don't often interfere though again I believe that some further felling would benefit the course.

You approach the club from the bustle of a dual carriageway but immediately are met by an air of calm and style. The clubhouse is very modern as it replaced the original 1939 building after a catastrophic fire in 2011. The original clubhouse was a delightful thatched building – this was common in Europe at the time and we will encounter a wonderful example in the next chapter – but the decision was taken not to try and copy the original style with the new building. It is one of the better examples I have seen of new clubhouses – sleek and stylish and very practical.

For some reason, golf-course clubhouses have a terrible record for being burned down. Without researching the topic, I can think of many that have suffered this fate. Perhaps the earliest was St. George's Hill in 1924 but more recently there has been Royal Mid Surrey, Machrihanish and Glasgow Killermont, while in 2022 we had within a few weeks of each other first Oakland Hills in the U.S. and then the brand-new Beaverbrook Club in Surrey. I wonder what has happened to insurance premiums since. How best to replace is a challenge. The only one above where I knew the original was Machrihanish and there is no doubt the new one is both architecturally and practically a huge improvement. The new Killermont has been restored to its original listed late-Georgian glory and I gather the plan at Oakland Hills is also to replace like-for-like. I never saw the old Royal Mid-Surrey clubhouse; the new one is very smart but many members say it lacks the character of the old. The bigger loss is often the contents and trophies which was certainly the case at Royal Mid-Surrey.

I was lucky to play Royal Sart-Tilman on a glorious day in early October – it was a bit early for autumn colour but it is likely to be magnificent in autumn as the trees are beautiful and they were just beginning to turn. The first two holes somewhat lull you into a false sense of what lies ahead. They are modest holes on flat land: a shortish, gentle dog-leg Par 4 followed by a slightly bland 140 yard Par 3. They are not bad holes just nothing very special. However, as you walk onto the 3rd tee all changes. For the next five holes, there is no more 'flat' as you are taken on a heady ride of dramatic elevation changes, both down and then up, often on the same hole. 3 and 4 play strongly downhill though the latter has a wide ravine which you need to carry just short of a raised green. 5 is a beast of a hole, stroke index 1 for a reason, as you play over another large ravine and then steeply uphill to a difficult green. I liked both the Par 5 7th, a right to left dog-leg over heavily undulating land and the Par 4 8th, which requires an accurate drive to enable a clear second shot into another raised green. 9 plays back to the clubhouse returning to the flatter land and is another Par 5 which I also liked, mainly because I hit my 9 iron third shot to about four feet and holed the putt for a rare birdie. All this in front of the Professional who was giving a lesson on the neighbouring putting green. I nodded to him as I walked past to the 10th tee, assuming an air of nonchalance, hopefully giving the impression that this was an everyday occurrence.

The 10th is a long Par 3 which plays across the front of the clubhouse – an intimidating shot with a large audience enjoying their drinks on the raised clubhouse terrace – and it provides me an opportunity to tackle the one caveat I have about the course. The hole is tough at about 190 yards (over 200 from the back tee), however, it has been designed with a steepish bank leading down to a shallow valley in front of a slightly raised green so shorter hitters could choose to run the ball in. However, the softness of the course is such that the only realistic way to hit the green is a full carry of over 180 yards. Yes, it was October and not July when I played but we had enjoyed one of the hottest and driest summers for many years and the ground was still too soft. I am no expert but I think it is because of the grasses used. It doesn't make it a bad hole – it just would be a better hole if you could hit the green with a choice of shot types.

11 and 12 are two great Par 4s with sloping fairways and tricky to hit greens and 13 is a delightful downhill Par 3 to a well-bunkered green. In truth, after this the course reverts to the more staid character of the opening holes with three Par 5s in the final five holes, the best being probably the 14th where the fairway narrows past an attractive pond just short of the green.

The course has 5 Par 3s, 5 Par 5s and 8 Par 4s.

The sylvan surroundings are a delightful place to play golf though it is not as peaceful as either Royal Antwerp or Royal Fagnes in Spa as, particularly on the front 9, there is road noise so you are aware that you are on the edge of a city. It's a bit like Walton Heath or that lovely corner around the turn of the Berkshire Blue with the modern world impinging on what otherwise would be perfect calm. The course is well looked after but is parkland rather than heathland and my impression is that it will get very soft in winter. This is a pity as it was not designed as a 'target' golf course and it would be enormous fun if the conditions were hard and dry. The course is a fine test though it would, in my view, be an even finer one if the turf could be firmed up. The clubhouse had a relaxed atmosphere with, as with Dinard, dining clearly taken seriously.

The Belgium Owl Distillery is situated near the village Fexhe-le-Haut-Clocher in Hesbaye just north of Liège. I mention Hesbaye as it is now a feature of the Owl's new bottle and label design with 'Distilled in Hesbaye' prominent on the front. Belgium is a complicated country with three political and administrative regions: Flanders in the north, Wallonia in the south and Brussels. Flanders is largely Dutch speaking and Wallonia French speaking. Flanders and Wallonia are then each divided into five provinces of which, in Wallonia, Liège is one. However, to an outsider it is even more confusing than that as one of Wallonia's regions is called Luxembourg, though that is different from Luxembourg the country which was split off back in 1839. Also, in this southern area of Belgium there are a number of German speakers who at times have asked for their own province. It is interesting to look at the map of the borders in the area; Liège is only 20 miles from Maastricht in the Netherlands, about 30 miles from Aachen in Germany and less than 50 miles from the border with Luxembourg. Indeed, the French border is only about 70 miles to the west. The area therefore is a good example of this tension between local identity, the nation state and bigger political institutions such as the EU. Maastricht was where the 1992 Treaty was signed which created the EU and paved the way for the Euro currency. I wonder whether it was chosen because of its peculiar geography, almost an enclave of the Netherlands surrounded by Wallonian, Belgium and Germany, to symbolise the big idea of creating EU citizenship.

The entrance to The Belgium Owl Distillery – the buildings had originally housed a convent

The Belgium Owl Distillery was set up by Etienne Bouillon in 2003. From a family of liquorists, he became interested in Scotch whisky and spent 10 years as an apprentice working on Islay with Jim McEwen at Bruichladdich. This association and friendship has been an important part of the development of the business. He created a vision of making a Belgium whisky working with local farmers and distilled his first product in 2003, bottling it in 2007. Shortly afterwards two big changes happened: he moved the distillery to large farm buildings surrounded by fields outside the nearby village of Fexhe-le-Haut-Clocher in 2010 and three years later replaced his old French stills with two from the recently closed Caperdonich Distillery at Rothes on Speyside. Caperdonich had been Glen Grant's second distillery but became a victim of industry rationalisation when Pernod Ricard closed it in 2002 only one year after buying it. These magnificent large stills were shipped from Edinburgh to Antwerp and onwards by road to their new home. The farm buildings, which apparently had previously also housed a convent, have been restored and also benefit from sitting above a spring from where the distillery extracts its water. The still house boasts a magnificent high barn ceiling which gives a real impression of scale. The location is part of Etienne's vision of a whisky with its own *terroir*. Barley all comes from the surrounding fields and hence the new prominence of 'Hesbaye' on the label. He has a partnership with 29 local farmers to secure sustainably grown barley. So Hesbaye relates to a purely geographical region and its '*terroir*' without any of the political or historical associations of Belgium or Wallonia. In this respect it is a similar approach to Armorik in Brittany, which emphasizes the geography and local climate, or indeed any of the Scotch whisky regions, e.g. Highland, Speyside, Lowland or Islay. There are no local maltings so this takes place in Zeeland in the Netherlands. The rest of the process is fairly traditional, using stainless steel for the mash tun and washbacks. Maturation and bottling are both undertaken on site with a new warehouse being introduced to meet the growing capacity.

There is a core range of four products, from 3- to 4-year-old year old whiskies matured in first-fill ex-Bourbon casks from Heaven Hill and bottled at 46% ABV. The range includes a single cask and a cask strength. A number of limited edition special whiskies, older and with fairly short sherry finishes, have been produced and by all accounts have sold out quickly. The business now exports ninety percent of its product. There is a small visitor centre with tours on certain days. The new bottle design with its 'owl-feathers look' is distinctive and a big improvement on the old, slightly utilitarian, shape and with the prominent 'Distilled in Hesbaye' communicates the local *terroir* proposition based on the barley and water source.

It is interesting to contrast the successes of Armorik and Belgium Owl which have both created quality products and a strong brand based on their distinctive localities with the Liber distillery in Spain which has tried but struggled to do the same. It seems the Spanish market is a difficult one to get a premium but that would not prevent an export-led strategy which the Owl has successfully implemented.

The classic wooded heathland at Eindhovensche. This is the second hole.

The delightful thatched clubhouse at Eindhovensche

CHAPTER FOUR

THE NETHERLANDS

'Whisky now belongs not to the Scots but to the world at large'

Aeneas MacDonald (aka George Malcolm Thomson 1899-1996)
Scottish journalist and author

THE FIRST 'WHISKY' distilled in the Netherlands was bottled as recently as 2007. However, genever or 'Dutch gin', which has been made for centuries, is a malted mash of cereals, redistilled with botanicals and then blended and aged so the process is not that different from Scotch whisky. So maybe it was not the Scots or the Irish who invented 'whisky' but the Dutch! The same is true of golf which some claim the Dutch also invented and witness 16th-century Flemish paintings which depict figures with sticks and balls. This was a game called 'colf' or 'kolf' and was generally played on ice and seems to have been a hybrid of what today we would understand as hockey and golf. There are other nationalities who could make similar claims: the Romans are known to have played a game called *paganica* with branches of trees and feather-stuffed leather balls, the French, a game called *jeu de maille,* a sort of long-distance croquet, while the Chinese during the 10th-century Song Dynasty had a game called *chuiwan* which involved hitting a ball with a stick while walking. Apparently, it was played with clubs which were inlaid with jade and gold so presumably was something of an elite sport. However, there were strong commercial links between Scotland and the Low Countries – the St Andrews Senzie Fair attracted many Dutch vessels and reciprocally Scottish merchants attended similar gatherings on the River Scheldt in Holland where it is likely that 'Scotch cleeks' and leather balls were traded. But while there are similarities there are also distinct differences as the Dutch game required the balls to be hit against posts or doors as opposed to into a hole. I don't think there is a definitive answer as to where 'golf' was invented – you can argue what constituted golf in those days in the same way as you can argue about what constitutes 'whisky' today. Mankind has probably played around with sticks and balls all over the world for many centuries just as mankind has looked to distil mashes of cereals in various formats.

Today the Netherlands cannot be deemed a thriving centre for either golf or whisky but what does exist is of high quality. There are a growing number of small whisky distillers but one business stands out – Zuidam – and it is this which we will visit. Dutch golf courses, as in many countries, can be divided into two categories: old classics, mainly the work of English designers, and modern 'stadium' type courses. Seven of the top eight (which would all appear in a European Top 50) are the former though some have changed locations since the formation of the clubs. Harry Colt is responsible for three: his famous links at Kennemer, near Zandvoort, and two heathland courses at Utretch de Pan and Eindhovensche. At all of these you will find exactly what you would expect from a Colt links or heathland classic in England including magnificent clubhouses. They are all in the 'must visit' category so my choice was eventually dictated by geography, Eindhovensche being the closest to Zuidam in the western side of the country.

Arguably one of Holland's greatest contributions to golf today is in fact a different drink from whisky. Kümmel, a clear herbal liqueur, flavoured with caraway seeds, cumin, fennel and orris, has become a firm favourite in many famous golf clubhouses, particularly Prestwick and Muirfield. It has been rumoured that Prestwick consumes an average of three cases a week.

The history of the spirit pre-dates modern golf, having been created by the distiller Lucas Bols in Holland in 1575. Over 100 years later it was discovered by the young Peter the Great of Russia on his trip to western Europe who then introduced it to his country where it became a favourite. Ludwig Mentzendorff then began producing it commercially in Riga in the 19th century. He started exporting to London around the mid-century and Mentzendorff remains one of the biggest brands today though it is now produced in France at the Combier distillery in the Loire Valley. There it is actually distilled from caraway seeds, rather than flavoured with them, in old stills designed by Gustav Eiffel, designer of the eponymous tower. The other main brand of kümmel associated with UK golf clubs is Wolfschmidt which also had its origins in Riga and was initially best known as a premium vodka brand favoured by James Bond in Ian Fleming's novels. Wolfschmidt kümmel is now produced in Holland by Beam Suntory, the multi-national spirits business and owner of the Teachers blended whisky brand as well as famous malts such as Laphroaig, Bowmore and Auchentoshan. There have, however, been recent worrying rumours that Beam have ended production.

It is funny how golf is associated with certain drinks. We encountered the famous Pink Jug at Royal Worlington, while kümmel is one of many drinks which I only consume at a golf club. About ten years' ago I won a bottle of kümmel as a prize at a golf day. I still have it today at home because while I enjoy kümmel, it only seems right to drink it after a game of golf – or rather before a game of golf because I usually have it as a digestif after a large lunch in order to fortify myself to face another 18 holes in the afternoon. It always makes me wonder whether the Wolfschmidt and Mentzendorff brand managers understand that an important segment of their target market are middle-aged, Scottish golfers looking to cleanse the palate after consuming a three-course lunch washed down with a bottle of claret.

There are other drinks I only have at a golf club. A Whisky Mac (a mixture of whisky and ginger wine apparently invented in India by a Colonel MacDonald) is more usually drunk before embarking on a round of golf on a cold, winter morning. Just in case non-golfers are thinking that golf is just an elaborate excuse to drink alcohol there are also many 'golfing' soft drinks; a *gunners* is a refreshing mix of ginger beer, ginger ale and angostura bitters. Others often associated with golf clubs are a *hillbilly*, a *rock shandy* and in Scotland a *John Panton* which as far as I can gather is just a Scottish *gunners*. There is some dispute about the exact make-up of ingredients for all these and they tend to vary regionally. Some mixture of ginger beer, ginger ale, grapefruit juice or lemonade and a dash of angostura usually meets the brief – Swinley Forest has its own recipe known as the *Swinley Special*. I'm not sure it matters greatly as long as they are refreshing, while their quaint names are very much part of the golfing experience.

I digress. Let's head for Eindhovensche, situated in a wooded expanse of heathland called 'Neiderheide' outside the town of Eindhoven which is possibly best known for being where one of Holland's most famous companies was formed – Philips Electronics. This is relevant because it was the brother of the Philips who formed the company who founded the golf club and succeeded in getting Harry Colt to design the course in 1928. The course was first played on in 1929 and the club, 'Eindhovensche Golf', founded in 1930. The clubhouse was designed to a 'country-house-style' brief by architects from Hilversum incorporating a dramatic leaded window designed by Joep Nicholas.

The clubhouse is very much the first thing to strike you as you arrive, a wonderful thatched building set within peaceful woodland. The area is a nature reserve and popular with walkers. Thatched clubhouses are something of a signature of Dutch courses with Colt's other two great creations, Utretcht and Kennemer also boasting them. We were grateful for the clubhouse as we arrived there on the hottest day of 2022 with temperatures heading to a peak of 38 degrees. The greeting was very welcoming but concern was expressed about whether we still wanted to play. Members had decided that discretion was the better part of valour and had stayed at home. However, we had travelled a long way for this treat and fortunately Colt had created Eindhovensche as two loops of 9 so we suggested that we would embark on the first 9, take a cooling break in the clubhouse, and then set out on the second 9. It was agreed that this was a sensible plan. So, after enjoying a cooling drink and a delicious, freshly made salmon salad we set out, armed with copious bottles of water, with the course to ourselves.

I think playing an exposed course with no trees would have been very difficult, but if there is anywhere to play in such temperatures, then Eindhovensche is a good candidate. The woods provided plenty of accessible shade and as the day progressed, a light breeze emerged which made the second 9 almost pleasant. The break after 9 holes was also a life saver. By the time we set out for the back 9, some members had decided that golf was possible and we were no longer alone.

How to describe the course? It is a heady mixture of Swinley Forest, Sunningdale and The Berkshire with perhaps a hint of Rosemount thrown in. Mainly tree-lined, giving each hole its definition, generally firm, sandy-soiled fairways (it was a hot July day), plenty of heather and bunkers to avoid and gentle rather than dramatic changes in elevation. While the lack of other players accentuated the quiet, this will always be a peaceful setting for golf. I particularly liked the frequent thatched roof small shelters set into the woods alongside the fairways. Everything at Eindhovensche is done with some style.

The routing is simple, consisting of two clockwise loops, the back 9 around a large lake which the clubhouse overlooks. Perhaps, unlike Hardelot for example, the course contains few truly memorable holes but instead they are consistently good. Everywhere there is understated quality; I enjoyed the short Par 4 2nd with its awkwardly positioned trees in the fairway and the 3rd is probably the best of the Par 3s, a long downhill shot of some 200 yards though this is balanced by the heavily bunkered short 8th. There are four good Par 5s, the final one of which, the 500-yard 17th, we managed to complete by hitting just 7 shots between us. A little explanation is required; I misjudged my second, hitting it, unusually, too well with the result that I caught a water hazard some 120 yards short of the green. I had to take a drop from where I hit the ball to 6 inches to make my five. (5 shots, 4 hits) My partner, hit two of his best shots ever to hit the green in two (yes, some 500 yards for an 8 handicapper) from where he holed from about 20 feet for an eagle. That might not sound that interesting but eagles are certainly worth a mention in my golfing circles.

After the round, Andrew (we are both Andrews, which makes life easy for opponents) celebrated his eagle by going wild-swimming in the lake. By that stage of the day a number of other locals had decided to cool off and do the same. The lake is geared up for this with platforms and pontoons. It is a very special place.

I really enjoyed the course but undoubtedly for me the highlight of Eindhovensche was the clubhouse. It is thatched but has been thoroughly modernised and is well-designed inside with changing areas downstairs and eating and club rooms upstairs, enjoying delightful views over the course and the lake. From the broad terrace you can see up or down the 1st, 9th 10th, 18th and across the lake, in the distance, the 16th. The clubhouse experience is a very important part of visiting a golf course and here Eindhovensche scores very, very highly. It serves food until around 9.30pm and the day we played members started appearing in the evening simply to enjoy the peaceful surroundings and excellent home-cooked food. We enjoyed fresh fish. The service was excellent, the ambience congenial rather than exclusive – there was a real 'club' feel to the place.

It is under an hour's drive to the village of Baarle Nassau. I talked in the last chapter about the interesting international geography of southern Belgium but Baarle Nassau is even more distinctive. There are actually two villages in one: Baarle Nassau, in the Netherlands, and Baarle Hertog which is part of Belgium (within the Province of Antwerp in Flanders) The Dutch/Belgium border is complicated and windy enough but Baarle Hertog comprises one hamlet called Zondereigen which is situated within the borders of Belgium and twenty exclaves which are totally surrounded by the Netherlands. Indeed, some of houses find themselves in two different countries. The complexity of the border apparently dates back to disputes between the Lords of Breda and the Dukes of Brabant in the medieval times. Matters were somewhat clarified by the Treaty of Maastricht in 1843 and have become less important since the Schengen Treaty and the creation of the EU at the more recent Maastricht Treaty. It was certainly an education for me. I learned about the difference between an enclave and an exclave as well as semi-enclaves and semi-exclaves, not to mention pene-exclaves all of which are too confusing to summarise here.

Let's return to the reason for my visit which was to visit the Zuidam Distillery, the oldest and biggest in the Netherlands. I had been kindly introduced to the Managing Director, Patrick van Zuidam, by Hans Offringa, a well-known writer who with his wife Becky call themselves *The Whisky Couple* and regularly write articles and books on whisky matters. Hans' book 'A Field Guide to Whisky' is an excellent guide to the product and the industry particularly for an amateur enthusiast. We all met on a bright autumn day at the distillery on the edge of the village. It was a very congenial morning, chatting about the business and whisky generally. Like golf, whisky provides common ground for fellow enthusiasts whatever their nationality. They were interested in my choice of distilleries in the other countries;

other whisky businesses are generally not seen as competitors but as fellow members of an international community.

The business was started back in 1974 by Patrick's father, Fred, producing liqueurs, genever, gin and vodka but it was Patrick who was behind the move into whisky during the late 1990s with the first Millstone single malt bottled in 2007. Whisky now accounts for about half the business. Patrick not only runs the business but is the master distiller and clearly now a very skilled one. I asked him how he learned his trade and he answered 'trial and error' which is surely a very honest answer. Certainly, he is self-taught but will have learned from many others across the industry. Whisky is that sort of industry. Zuidam has developed from a small family business set up by a working-class family where everyone mucked in to become an internationally respected industry player.

Zuidam does not have a visitor centre – the business is all about the products. What then are the distinctive approaches to distilling whisky which Patrick espouses? They use local grain which is now quite common amongst start-up distilleries and until recently the barley was milled in windmills. They still have arrangements with four windmills but because they have grown there is not enough capacity for all their grist to be made in this way. The pot stills are from Forsyths and are large and tall but otherwise quite conventional though the inside of the wash still has been modified so that it can handle rye distillation. Where I, as a layman, see a difference in the approach is in the fermentation in the washbacks. Patrick is very particular about the blend of yeasts and uses a mix of brewers' and distillers' yeasts. This in itself is not that unusual but what is surprising is the near seven-day fermentation time which I don't think I have come across elsewhere and which Patrick sees as central to his product. He is of the view that this gives time for flavour to develop and any oncosts in the time of doing this plus the lower yields it produces is a price worth paying. The washbacks are also temperature-controlled, again something I have not encountered elsewhere. This is an admirable approach to product quality and distinctiveness.

A Pedro Ximenex sherry cask at Zuidam used for their Millstone whisky

He also has strong views on maturation and here his fondness for sherry casks is clear, be they of American or European oak. From looking around the warehouse, Pedro Ximenex oloroso seems to be a favourite. I ask about the competition for sourcing quality sherry casks and he replies with a twinkle in his eye that his wife is Spanish so he has good contacts – this may account for his love of sherry maturation. He makes clear that his use of sherry casks is not for finishing – it's all or nothing. As well as experimenting with cask types and ages, he is now releasing some 10- 20-year-old aged editions and some peated versions with barley from Scotland. He also looking at rye whisky which he manages to distil in the same equipment despite the challenges which that poses. Rye is not as easy to handle as barley. I have read good reviews of this product from experts.

Zuidam's single malt whisky brand is Millstone and I love the story of how this came about. He was about to launch his whisky under the brand 'Lowlands' which he felt was a good name for the first Dutch whisky as it seemed to combine a characteristic of the Netherlands with a hint of a Scotch whisky region. On the Friday afternoon before the launch the following week he received a letter from lawyers representing a well-known music festival which was also called 'Lowlands' claiming a trademark breach. He was dubious about their claim but was faced with the prospect of a tortuous legal battle with the attendant bills, not an attractive prospect for a small business. He made a decision to think of an alternative and following a quick brainstorm came up with 'Millstone' as it represented his distinctive milling of the barley in a windmill. Using a graphics package on his laptop he knocked up some labels and the following week Millstone was introduced to the market. That is the way to react to unpredicted adversity.

There is so much to admire in the business but I think the core of the success is Patrick's focus on product quality – this has been more of a product-quality led success than a marketing one though clearly sales and marketing are now being developed as the business has grown. I have talked before about my novice status in whisky appreciation and how my tastes have developed during the course of my research. I started with a preference for the milder, lowland malts, have developed more recently a liking for a bit of peat flavour – occasionally, depending on my mood – but I have to say that you can't beat a good sherry-matured whisky and Millstone is an excellent example.

I have stated before that I don't like having either favourite golf courses or favourite whiskies – who would want only to play one golf course or drink one whisky for the rest of their lives – but four countries into this tour I have probably experienced my favourites so far of both in the Netherlands. Maybe the Dutch did invent them both after all.

This little house overlooking the fairway at Menaggio and Cadenabbia Golf Club on Lake Como adds to the charm of the surroundings.

The extraordinary Puni Distillery building in the Italian Tyrol won an architectural award

CHAPTER FIVE

ITALY

'Civilization begins with distillation'

William Faulkner (1897-1962)

American Writer and Nobel Prize laureate

ITALY IS PERHAPS a surprise inclusion in this book as it is neither renowned for its golf courses nor its whisky distilleries. Indeed, at time of writing it had only one whisky distillery, Puni in the Tyrol, and it was this in particular that encouraged me to include a chapter on Italy as Puni is an impressive business. Italy has also begun to make its mark on golf with Francesco Molinari's popular victory at The Open at Carnoustie in 2019 and Italy being awarded The Ryder Cup in 2023. This will take place at Marco Simone on a newly designed layout at a country club developed in the 1970s in the countryside outside Rome. I was keen, however, to visit a smaller club and I wanted some geographical proximity to Puni.

I am not sure whether Italy suffers from a lack of natural golfing terrain. There are no links courses (though Venezia, situated on the southern tip of the Venice Lido, has some linksy characteristics) and there are very few courses of note south of Rome. In the main there are country clubs around Rome, others in Tuscany around Florence while the other main concentration of good courses is in and around Milan and the Italian Lakes. The oldest club in Italy is Ugolino near Florence which was founded in 1889 but moved to its current, very picturesque, location in 1934. Ugolino was one of a number of courses designed by the English who felt that cultural Grand Tours of Italy would be considerably enhanced by having good golf courses to play. They also built tennis courts and even cricket pitches. The equivalent of Ugolino in Rome is Acquasanta which was laid out in 1902 in a delightful setting just off the Via Appia Antica to the south-east of the city. Both these would be good candidates for their settings and rich history but there are as yet no signs of whisky-making in Tuscany or Lazio.

Italy's top-rated course is Circolo Villa D'Este near Lake Como but this ultra-exclusive club, though it dates back to the 1920s and has held The Italian Open a dozen times, doesn't really fit my criteria. However, on the other side of Lake Como is Menaggio and Cadenabbia Golf Club which also dates from the 1920s and is a much more understated and charming version of Villa d'Este.

Asked to name three Italian golfers most people would go for Constantino Rocca and the Molinari bothers. Rocca was famous for holing a 60-foot putt on the 18th green at St Andrew's in 1995 to force himself into a play-off with John Daly, which he lost. He was also the first Italian to play in The Ryder Cup. The Molinaris came to prominence when they played together in the 2010 Ryder Cup in Wales – Francesco had qualified for the team and the Captain, Colin Montgomerie, added brother Eduardo as one of his 'picks'. In recent years, Francesco began to perform increasingly successfully both in Europe and the US, culminating in his Open triumph. It is too early to judge the extent this success plus the Ryder Cup will have on the popularity of golf in Italy though there are signs of a number of young Italian stars emerging and it was good to see Felippo Celli win the silver medal for the leading amateur at the 150th Open St. Andrew's in 2022. Today golf still has the reputation, as in many European countries, of being something of an elite sport but maybe the Ryder Cup will change this.

When I mentioned Lake Como to friends there were always the same two things mentioned: its beauty and the fact that George Clooney lived there. I can't vouch for the latter but the former is certainly true. I flew into Milan whence it is only a 40-minute drive up to the bottom of the lake. Lake Como is distinctively shaped like a walking two-legged figure with the town of Como sitting at the base of the western leg and Lecco at the foot of the eastern one. I drove up the west coast of the western leg through Moltrasio, Argegno, Lenno and Tremezzina. The narrow lake with steep mountains to each side is indeed spectacularly beautiful. Mennagio is just beyond the meeting of the two legs where the main and widest section of the lake starts. We will come to the golf club in a moment but any visit, for whatever reason, must take time to savour the beauties all around. Perhaps the best spot is around Tremezzina which looks out over to the pretty village of Bellagio which is situated on the apex of the promontory where the two legs join – the figure's crotch if you like. This is the point to take a ferry out onto the lake and stop off at one of the many hotels or cafes at Bellagio and enjoy the calming views of the lake with small ferry boats criss-crossing it, operating to an appropriately fluid, Italian-style, timetable. It was said that Mussolini was responsible for getting the Italian trains to run on time; this, in my experience, doesn't apply to Lake Como ferries but frankly no one seems to care as minor delays enable you to glory in the splendour of the surroundings for a little longer.

The two most impressive buildings on the west coast are probably The Grand Hotel Tremezzo and the famous Villa Carlotta. The Grand Hotel is an imposing and achingly beautiful art nouveau classic, set in lush gardens and commanding an unsurpassed view over the lake to Bellagio. It was built in 1910 and while it was commandeered as an army clinic during the Great War, it resumed its role as a popular hotel location for the rich and famous thereafter and remains so today. If your budget does not allow you to stay there you should at least drop in for an admittedly expensive coffee and enjoy a stroll around its gardens and take in the views. Almost next door is the equally famous Villa Carlotta built at the end of the 17th century by the Marquis Giorgio Clerici of Milan. Its magnificent botanical gardens are world famous and it also hosts many art collections. A few miles away is the small village of Giulino di Mezzegra which, depending on how you look at it, has a more disturbing history being the site of the execution of Benito Mussolini and his mistress Claretta Petacci.

Menaggio and Cadenabbia Golf Club is less than 15 minutes' drive from here. As you drive along the lake, you wonder where the golf course could be. Entering Menaggio, just before the main road goes into a long tunnel, you turn left up the side of the mountains. The main road is steep and narrow and will eventually take you over to Porlezza at the top end of Lake Lugarno. It's only about ten miles but the road means it is a slow journey. For the golf club, however, you turn off this 'main' road and climb even more steeply up an even narrower road (indeed the tightness of the road is a portent for the fairways which are to follow) by way of some fairly dramatic hairpin bends – these will become a feature of this Italian chapter. All the time you are thinking that you must have taken a wrong turning because there cannot possibly be a golf course up there. You must, however, persevere as you soon turn off into the golf club and find yourself parking outside a handsome building with delightful views of the lake, this time from a considerable height. There is a complex of buildings and a short inspection quickly reveals a tee box with a narrow fairway plunging down amidst pine trees. Yes, someone had decided to build a golf course in this seemingly impossible place.

The club has an extremely relaxed and unpretentious feel to it. The main part of the lovely clubhouse is a large bar area and restaurant which is central to the club. The changing rooms are downstairs and here you find yourself in what looks like the locker room of a very traditional British golf club with delightful old wooden lockers and opulent porcelain wash areas. The urinals alone are worth the visit. The atmosphere is certainly 'clubby' and there is everything which you would expect to see at a traditional British club: pictures of past captains, historical golf pictures, trophies and old clubs. Menaggio and Cadenabbia even has its own golf library of which it is very proud.

The origins of the club are very 'English' being founded in 1907 by an English banker, Henry Mylis and three colleagues. They identified the site in the hills above Menaggio and built a course of 9 holes which was extended to 18 in 1919. The club remained English-owned until it was purchased in 1961 by the Roncoroni family. John Harris, whose company had a worldwide reputation for building golf courses and was involved in the design or reconfiguration of a number of Italian courses, was commissioned to redesign the course in 1965.

Perhaps one aspect of the club which is less obviously 'English' is the restaurant which is quite 'high end' serving homemade pastas and many Italian delicacies. The day I visited, most of the people I saw in the clubhouse had come for the food rather than the golf.

I cannot claim that it is a great golf course but nor is it an ordinary one. Its location makes it anything but ordinary. It's like Boat of Garten but except for the Cairngorms you have the Alps. I like courses where there is both primary and secondary beauty; the primary beauty is the ambience of the tree-lined fairways and the local environment while the secondary beauty is when you lift your eyes to admire the distant views. At Boat of Garten the natural bumpy fairways amidst the silver birches are complemented by the majestic longer vistas across the Cairngorms. It's the same at Menaggio; there is plenty to admire with the pretty tree-lined, undulating fairways while all the time you are surrounded by dramatic snow-capped mountains in the distance.

Putting aside for a moment its spectacular location, the golfing challenge is significant. At around 6,000 yards off the back tees, it is not long but the holes are by necessity quite tight as the 18 holes have been designed into a relatively small acreage. As a result, the tee shots have to be accurate and with the greens being small the approach shots also require considerable thought. The course is obviously closed for at least three months over the winter so the turf is hardly perfect for golf yet in the summer it can get quite hard and dry which will increase the premium on accurate shot-making.

The layout is that of two nines which return to the clubhouse. There are five Par 3s and three Par 5s. The first hole plays sharply downhill and is followed by two consecutive Par 3s, the first played slightly uphill to a plateau green and the second sharply downhill. A tricky short Par 4 follows requiring a carefully placed tee shot to give a clear site of the green. The only Par 5 on the front 9 follows with the third shot to the raised green being suitably testing with a sharp fall off area to the left. The 6th plays again further downhill from where holes 7-9 climb steeply back to the clubhouse.

After the climb you may need a refreshment at the halfway hut which greets you on the walk to the 10th which is a very tight Par 3. The back nine repeats the pattern with holes leading you down the hill though this time there are five holes to get you back. The Par 5 13th is the extent of the course and here the views of the Alps in the background are at their most magnificent.

It was on the back nine that I met and joined up with Geoff, an American member of the club from California who had bought a house locally and spends the summers on Lake Como. Geoff took his game seriously and reached the final two Par 4s requiring a Par on each to beat his personal course record. These two holes are on the face of it quite friendly, two Par 4s of under 300 yards. He advised a five iron off the tee on both. The 17th tee shot is blind. Yes, all that is required is a five iron and a wedge and if you hit both of them straight you should make 4. The problem is that if you don't, you may easily take 6 – which is what Geoff did on 17 much to his annoyance. He then made a 5 on 18 so his personal best wasn't even challenged. I made a solid 4 at 17 and hit a very satisfying 5 iron to the centre of the 18th fairway but then spent too much time worrying about how any shot hit slightly right looked as if it would run steeply off the green into the overlooking bar. The result was that I inevitably pulled my wedge and hit the path to the left of the green. I never saw the ball again.

Menaggio and Cadenabbia is a proper golf club and I am not sure how many similar ones there are in Italy. My suspicion is that most others are either elite Country Clubs or modern resort-style facilities. I have nothing particular against either of these but it is smaller genuine clubs which I prefer. I have one concern about the club. Everything I saw about it made me feel it was a club I would enjoy being a member of until I read this on its website. On its '*Rules for Visitors*' it says the following: '*The Competition Committee has decided that the time limit to play our course is four hours and thirty minutes.*' Four and a half hours to play a 6,000 yard course? That's over 20 minutes per hole. There are five Par 3s. How can you take that long? The small bit of land means that there are seldom long walks between the greens and the next tee except after the 14th where, strangely, you have to walk across the neighbouring 12th fairway to find the 15th tee. I can only assume that this advisory time allowance provides for stopping for a plate of Spaghetti Carbonara and a Peroni (other Italian beer brands are available) at the halfway hut.

You might expect me again to rile against slow play. It is good to see that the game's authorities are beginning to take it more seriously and starting to penalise professionals. As I have said before, it really is daft that one of golf's main downsides is that it takes too long to play in this time-poor world we live in, yet increasingly those who play it, play unnecessarily slowly. I believe it will help if the professional game speeds up and the new law changes have helped in this respect. Yet when you read that in the 1926 Open at Royal Birkdale, Walter Hagan was criticised for taking three hours to complete his round you wonder what has happened. In those days the last two rounds of The Open were both played on the final day, with four hours allowed between the allotted tee times – this was 'to allow players time to go back to their hotels for lunch in between rounds'.

The elegant and distinctively designed Puni whisky bottle

Googlemaps told me that the drive to Puni Distillery at Glurns in the Italian Tyrol was about three hours. There follows a story about the dangers of Googlemaps (again, other brands of journey mapping are available). I looked to book the one hotel in the small, attractive looking town of Glurns where the distillery is located but it was fully booked for the days I wanted to go. Instead, I decided to break the journey and head for Bormio, a ski resort at the foot of the Alps which I had heard was a pleasant place to stay at and so it proved. The drive to Bormio from Menaggio was perhaps less scenic than I had expected (the top end of Lake Como does not have the same charm as the southern end and the road north from the top of the lake to Bormio via Tirano is rather bland). In fact, the direct route to Glurns would take you further north via St Moritz in Switzerland and is much more scenic. Here it is very much 'The Sound of Music' landscape where the cows really do have bells round their necks. Bormio, however, is worth a visit even out of the ski season. It is a prettily situated medieval town with plenty of bars and restaurants. And Googlemaps will tell you that the Puni distillery at Glurns is just 30 miles away. Perfect. Closer inspection tells you that the journey will take an hour and 10 minutes. Well, that's fine. Wait a minute; 70 minutes to do less than 30 miles? That's an average speed of just over 25 miles an hour. Strange.

There is a reason for this. Glurns is in fact, as the crow flies, less than 25 miles away. The problem is that there is a mountain range in between and you have to climb up to 7,000 feet (and down again) in between. This is done by way of a series of extreme switchbacks all the way up and all the way back down. The hairpin bends I described on the way up to Mennagio Golf Club are nothing by comparison. I can tell you now that an average speed of 25 miles an hour is vastly overstating what is safe.

This is Italy and safety barriers are at best intermittent. I set out on a bright morning but by the top it was grey and sleety. The road was damp. Yes, it was dramatic but it was drama that I could have done without. And my eyes seldom had the opportunity to leave the inadequately wide road immediately ahead of me. The 29 miles took me over an hour and a half and I arrived in Glurns with some relief but still a nervous wreck. I certainly needed a whisky. In future I will examine Googlemaps in a little more detail.

Glurns is an attractive little town in the Vinschgau valley. There is a lively hotel in the main square and a number of shops and cafes but it is small. The distillery is situated on a small industrial estate on the edge of the town – not an attractive site in itself but there is always in this area the impressive backdrop of the Ortler mountains.

Even more impressive though is the building, a dramatic looking copper-coloured lattice cube, 13 metres by 13 metres, which certainly stands out from its neighbouring buildings which were all what you might expect on a small light industrial estate. The offset red bricks were apparently inspired by a traditional local style of barn buildings. And the statement which the building makes is very much the statement which Puni wants to make in the market. Puni is proper malt whisky, Italian style. The Italian style is the role that design plays throughout the business, from the distinctive building and the quite radical bottle design to the smart visitor centre and even the layout of the various production processes. Design and 'look' are seen as important and play a central role in the business to a much greater extent than I have seen anywhere else. As its website declares: '*The Puni cube reflects the interplay of tradition and modernity at Puni distillery and its way of life: modern, elegant and venturous.*'

The distillery was set up by the Ebensperger family in 2010. Albrecht Ebensperger was a builder with a passion for Scotch whisky who felt that the local area, with a tradition of growing grain (though mainly rye), a relatively dry climate and ample water supplies water from the Puni river, was a perfect place to start an Italian whisky distillery. He engaged an architect friend to create the magnificent building – it has subsequently won an architectural award – and had the pot stills specifically designed by Forsyths to his own exacting requirements. Intriguingly, the brief was for the wash still and the spirit still to look exactly the same from the outside while obviously doing their slightly different jobs inside – so that there was symmetry to the design of the layout in the distillery. The first whisky was then produced in 2012 and releases have been made since 2015.

There are a number of elements that make Puni whisky distinctive. To begin with, their mash bill is generally a mix of barley, wheat and local rye, all malted. No peat is used. The washbacks are made from local larch wood and the fermentation time a relatively long 96 hours. The distilling process is also quite unique, using overheated water to heat the stills which they claim allows very precise temperature control and thereby enables careful selection of spirit quality. Maturation is in a dunnage-style warehouse nearby and the difference here is the local climate which has extremes of cold winters and hot summers. This causes an accelerated maturation so they claim that their five- year-old whisky is equivalent to a normal eight-year-old. The local angel gets a generous 8% in these climatic conditions. As with any new distillery they are still experimenting and are also storing spirit for longer periods inside underground military bunkers where the humidity is higher and the temperature constant. The main wood used is ex-bourbon casks and these are supplemented with Masala casks from Sicily and wine casks (generally Pinot Nero) from the South Tyrol both of which give an Italian twist to a traditional process. While they don't use peat, they are doing some finishing in Islay casks to meet this sector of the market. They are now also producing some whisky from malted barley only.

The scale of the operation is small and they do not see volume as important. The vast majority of sales are in Italy. Another Italian feature was that I noticed locks on every part of the process, not just the spirit safe as you would see in the UK; apparently, every production run has to be supervised by two customs inspectors. I thought they were joking at first but it is true. Their production planning process requires them to ensure that the inspectors can be present but they cheerfully say that they have a good relationship with their local inspectors and it is rarely a problem. This sounds very Italian to me.

The design of the stills at Slyrs echo the local church architecture in Bavaria.

The new links at Budersand on the island of Sylt

CHAPTER SIX

GERMANY

'Unlike the other Scotch game of whisky drinking, excess in it is not injurious to health'

Sir Walter Simpson (1843-1898)
Scottish Philosopher and author of The Art of Golf

IT IS ONLY just over a three-hour drive to our next location, across the border into Austria, past Innsbruck and then into Bavaria in Germany. However, this is a journey probably best experienced in summer or else the Alpine geography could easily get the better of you. Germany was a dilemma for me; the largest country in Europe, I felt that I had to explore its relationship with golf and whisky but neither are mainstream activities. Germany has produced two major golf champions, Bernhard Langer and Martin Kaymer, but in truth for a country of its size, the choice of courses is disappointing. Only five courses in Germany feature in Europe's Top 100 and only one dates back to before 1940. This is the Hamburger Club which was built by Colt, Alison and Morrison in the 1930s and is the top-ranked course in the country. While there is no shortage of distilleries producing whisky – maybe 60-70 across the country – most of these have whisky as a relatively recent add-on. There are a few exceptions. St Kilian, near Frankfurt, for example, is very much looking to be a malt whisky specialist in the Scottish mode. The area of greatest concentration is in Bavaria, perhaps not surprising given its strong beer-brewing tradition, but here, while there are many golf courses and some inevitably very scenic ones, the turf doesn't lend itself to golfing greatness. Having compromised on this in Italy, I felt I had to look at other options. The north of Germany has a long coastline and has some interesting links courses, both old and new. The oldest is a nine-hole course on one of the Friesan islands in the North Sea, Nordenay, which dates from the 1920s. I was most amused to read on its website the definition of 'links' which it explains is nothing to do 'with directional information' (the German word 'links' meaning left). There is another nine-hole links course even further north at St. Peter-Ording on the coast. This was designed by Frank Pennink in the 1970s. But undoubtedly the best course is a new links on the island of Sylt, Germany's most northerly point.

That is my dilemma; the best courses are in the north of Germany and the best distilleries are in the south. So, as in Spain, I change my own rules – because I can. In Germany we will visit one of the most southerly distilleries in the country at Slyrs (about ten miles from the Austrian border) and one of the most northerly golf courses in the country, Budersand, on the island of Sylt. There are 700 miles between the two so about a 12-hour drive! While I suggest that the trip to Sylt is therefore best combined with visits in chapters 7 and 8 to the relatively nearby Denmark and southern Sweden, there is in fact now an easy transport option from Munich; the Alpine-Sylt express runs twice weekly overnight. It actually starts in Salzburg but takes about 14 hours from Munich. The concept is very similar to the recently upgraded Caledonian Express from London which takes you to various locations in Scotland. And crucially there is another connection between Slyrs Distillery and Sylt which we will learn about.

Slyrs Distillery is situated just outside the pretty town of Schliersee on the lake of the same name in the foothills of the Bavarian Alps. It is in a modern, attractively designed, wooden building on the main road with a large shop and substantial 'Caffee/Lunchery' well set-up for visitors. While the distillery is a purpose-built whisky-focused operation it was set up by the Stetter family, owners of the Lantenhammer Distillery in nearby Hausham which has been producing local fruit spirits since 1928. When Florian Setter took over the family business during the 1990s, he made a trip to Scotland and was struck by the similarities between the Highlands of Scotland and Bavaria – mountains, clear water and pure air – and decided to set about producing a Bavarian single malt. They began by producing whisky in their old distillery and then built the new distillery on the south side of Schliersee in 2007. The visitor centre and the 'Caffee' and 'Lunchery' followed in 2016.

The name 'Slyrs' is rooted in Bavarian history and has connections with Ireland and Scotland. It was the name of a monastery founded in the area in 779 by five Scottish and Irish monks near Schliersee. The original monastery was moved in the 12th century to the site of the current St. Sixtus parish church in the town and then relocated in 1495 to the Frauenkirche, the famous cathedral in Munich. The St. Sixtus church, built in the early 18th century, sits in a beautiful location overlooking the lake, is an impressive example of ecclesiastical baroque architecture and is well worth a visit. Bavaria itself is an outstandingly beautiful area with, like Scotland, many distinctive local characteristics, be it the topography of the land, accent and dialect, culture and food. Certainly, a menu in Bavaria will read very differently than a menu in, say, Hamburg. One new local delicacy which I came across was the wonderfully named 'Kaiserschmarm', roughly translated as 'King's Nonsense'. This comprises a large plate of broken up pancakes (be sure to get the proper version with raisins) which you dip in an apple sauce. It's a sort of Bavarian version of Eton Mess. Apparently, it derives from the infamous King Ludwig arriving unannounced at a hostelry which had very little available food and the only thing they were able to conjure up hurriedly was pancakes and apple sauce, rather messily presented by an anxious landlord. King Ludwig, however, was delighted with it and it became everyone's favourite. It certainly fills a space after a day of skiing or walking in the Bavarian mountains.

You can pre-book tours at the distillery for groups or you can just wander around yourself following a series of numbered boards which explain the process. The equipment is modern (stainless steel mash tun and washbacks) and German built. The stills are distinctive with their bases encased in attractive brickwork and the necks topped with an onion-shaped dome rather reflective of the catholic church architecture of the region – the 'zweibeltürme', or 'onion-towers'. Mashing, fermentation and distillation all take place in the same room. There is then a large room impressively displaying maturing barrels with a galleried tasting-area which enjoys magnificent views up the valley to the Bavarian Alps.

Barley from northern Bavaria is used and the fermentation process is relatively long followed by double distillation and non-chill filtering. Much is made of the unique, pure Bavarian water which is used for diluting – again the relevance of the type of water used in the main process remains a mystery to me. What is interesting is the use of virgin American oak casks for initial maturation and the core 'Classic' product reflects this. It is pleasant and mild but perhaps lacking anything more than that. A range of products finished in other casks are part of an extensive range – sherry, oloroso, port, marsala, amontillado, madeira and sauternes. I have not tried any of these but I did enjoy their '51 Edition', a mix of sherry, port and sauternes finishes, which was certainly a more complex product. However, I do have a favourite which is their 'Mountain Edition' matured in a small warehouse, 1501 metres up on the top of Stümpling mountain. This is something no Scotch could ever do – Ben Nevis is a mere 1435 metres high. The empty casks were transported up by chairlift (one barrel per chair) and filled at the top in a new purpose-built mountain warehouse. I had to go and see for myself. The views from the top of Stümpling are magnificent and it is a popular skiing spot. You can look through the window into the warehouse and, fortunately, try the whisky in the neighbouring mountain-top restaurant. I have always wondered about the effect of different storage conditions for maturation on the flavour outcomes. I remember at Bunnahabhain being told that storage by the sea gave it a 'salty' taste from the sea air, something I was not convinced about. But I can understand the chemistry of the effect which extremes of temperature can have – at this altitude the temperature changes both during the day and across the seasons are dramatically greater than anything you would get in Scotland – this effect had been mentioned both in Granada in Spain and Puni in Italy. The effect is to speed up maturation which is generally a good thing. Maybe it was the context, a beautiful clear day with a cloudless sky, but I found this whisky had that perfect combination of smoothness combined with a depth of 'whisky' flavour. This tells me that maturation (format, cask-type, environment, time) really is everything when it comes to whisky outcomes. But so is the context of when and where and with whom you are tasting it.

I am not finished with whisky and Slyrs in this chapter but for now we must head north.

There are a number of reasons for choosing Sylt, the farthest rather than the nearest golf course in Germany from the Slyrs distillery. The following chapters cover Scandanavia so we are headed in the right direction. Sylt is a very beautiful island, in a very different way from Bavaria, and since 2009 has boasted a top-class golf course and, as we will see, there is another reason: on the island's most northerly tip there is a very direct connection with the Slyrs distillery which we have just visited. I will return to that later.

The main transport route from Germany to Sylt is a car train from the northern town of Niebull. There is no need to book the service; there are regular trains and you just turn up and wait for the next one. You drive the car onto the train and it takes you across the mudflats on a causeway onto the central part of the island. The scenery is not spectacular – it is too flat for that – but there is a sense of excitement and adventure as you approach the island. The train comes into the main town on the island, Westerland, which is situated in its central section. Sylt is shaped like an open crab claw, running south to north with a thin arm and then the large open claw in the north. While the island is pretty, Westerland is not particularly so. It is where the island's services are concentrated – shops, a small airport, train station, big hotels. To get to Budersand you need to head to the southernmost tip, a journey of some 25 minutes. It is an engaging journey along a very straight road banked by high dunes so that you do not really get a view of the coast though for most of the journey the island is only about half a mile across.

The tasting room at Slyrs has extensive views up the valley to the Bavarian Alps

There are some 25 miles of beaches on Sylt. As you approach the tip and the small town of Hornum, it broadens a little and this is where Budersand is situated. There is a large harbour and a rather unattractive looking hotel but just behind it on the eastern side is a large area of linksland where the course has been built. It is one of those pieces of land which seem to be destined to be a golf course and which if it had been in Scotland you would think would have been a golf course a long time ago. However, it turns out that the land had been occupied by a barracks and a seaborne military base during the war. It had been abandoned some years ago and left an unattractive and ghostly presence with many derelict buildings and extensive unkept paved roads. In 2004 the golf-course architect Rolf-Stephan Hansen persuaded the entrepreneur Claudia Ebert to invest in creating a golf course there. New projects such as this are seldom approved on Sylt but as the area was something of an eyesore the locals saw the benefits. The project was undertaken to strict environmental standards and it removed many acres of contaminated land. The course opened in 2008 and the hotel was added in 2009. I said that the hotel is not a particularly attractive building and we didn't stay there, but by all accounts it has a very good reputation for both the standard of accommodation and its restaurant.

There are three other courses on Sylt so Budersand is very much the newcomer but it is in a class of its own. You park by the hotel and have to walk up a hill to the clubhouse which is situated in a fine position overlooking the course but which has a utilitarian rather than welcoming feel about it. The course is privately owned and there is a small club membership limited to 50 people. The club partners closely with the hotel and green fees are easy to obtain. I suppose the proximity of the hotel means that there is limited use for extensive clubhouse facilities but it is a little disappointing for the visitor.

Any sense of disappointment however is left in the clubhouse because the course is a masterpiece. It is a perfect piece of land on which to design a golf course but nonetheless the design is impressive and there are no weak holes and many great ones. The first four holes cover the spectrum: the first, a long Par 4, starts from an elevated tee where you need an accurate drive down to a dog-leg from where the hole plays back uphill to a green nestling high in the dunes; the second is a short Par 4 playing sharply downhill but again accuracy is required; the 3rd is a long Par 5 playing downhill and sweeping right to left to a green at the northern end of the course; the fourth is a Par 3 with a well- protected green. Every hole from there onwards fits into one of these categories; tough long Par 4s, tricky shorter ones, Par 3s of different lengths, all well-protected, and good solid Par 5s. It is difficult to know which holes to feature but just as the first four holes excite, so too do the final four. The 15th is the shortest of the Par 3s and is a pretty hole playing down to a tricky green just above the beach. There follow two long Par 5s, both over 500 yards and playing in opposite directions, so whatever the wind direction one will play with the wind and the other against. They also feature ditches which make them more than just long-hitting holes – a degree of strategy is required. The final hole is then a 400 yard plus Par 4 with a sharp right to left dog-leg requiring an accurate tee shot to enable a clear shot uphill to the final green.

I am not surprised that Budersand is ranked so highly. It is a magnificent golf course and an exceptional design. The course is well kept and the links turf was in fine condition when we played in August. The layout requires very accurate play as much of the heavy rough is termed 'Biotope', an environmentally protected area from where you have to take a drop so effectively a hazard or, in the new parlance following the recent rule changes, a 'penalty area'. Even the areas of the rough which are not penalty areas are either the tricky links marram grass or thick straggly heather-like plants which even your 9 iron will find a challenge. The sea is very much a background feature –the closest you get to the coast is the green on the short 15th – but clearly the wind is a major factor as you would expect on a links course.

With reference to the new rules and terminology ('penalty areas' rather than 'hazards'), it is interesting how changes to the rules bring about unintended consequences. I think it is a rule of life that most innovations do this and sometimes these consequences are good and sometimes not so good. I support most of the new rules as they were intended to simplify the rules and to speed up play and for the most part they have done just that. There are probably, as with any changes, some modifications to be made. The dropping of the ball from the knee and not the shoulder was intended to be both fairer and to speed up play. However, penalising someone who, after years of having to drop from the shoulder, mistakenly does so is daft particularly as it confers no advantage.

One of the biggest changes was being allowed to leave the pin in on the green. I think this was a good innovation though it has not turned out quite as expected and has given rise to a whole new aspect of the game: flag etiquette. The intention was to allow the flag in for long putts thereby saving time – if one player is off the green and plays first, the other who is ready to putt doesn't have to wait to have the flag attended, this saves a significant amount of time. However, the rule allows players to have the flag in for any length of putt, even short ones. The problem here is that some people prefer to putt with the flag in and others with it out. As in everything – rather like 'big-endians and little-endians' in *Gulliver's Travels* with regard to which end of a boiled egg you should break into – there are militant wings on both sides of the debate. I admit I tend towards the latter – if I can see the hole, I find the flag a distraction especially if it is flapping in the wind or there is a shadow across your line. This can lead to problems and the opposite effect of actually slowing up play. A player who likes the flag out from ten feet is followed by a player who likes it in from four feet who then has to take the flag back out for the 'outer' to hole his two-footer. Some of the militant 'inners' grumble at this – why bother putting the flag back? 'Just keep it in all the time' they say. The short-term Covid rule change which required the flag to be left in at all times was of course a triumph for 'inners' while 'outers' like myself had to get used to it.

It seems to me that 'flag etiquette', as with all etiquette, is important. The law change is good because for the most part it saves time. However, it is necessary to respect both 'outers' and 'inners' and I have to say that I have felt pressure from some militant 'inners' to keep the flag in for short putts. This is I think unfair. Equally if someone likes to put the flag back in, you should be aware of this and help accordingly though I have to say that I find it bewildering to see someone ask, as I have experienced, for it to be put back in for a 3-foot putt. But flag etiquette is simply an extension of overall etiquette which requires every player not just to think of their own preferences but to acknowledge those of their playing companions, just as you should not only be aware of where you have hit your shot but also that of your companion. Simply asking at the beginning of the game how your partner likes the flag and acceding to this rather than imposing your preference is all that is required. Again, this is not a bad model for how to live your life off the golf course. Sermon over.

Budersand would surely be a very well-known course were it not for its remote location. In this respect it suffers like some of the more remote Irish links, Rosapenna in Donegal for example, from being difficult, and expensive, to get to. But it is certainly worth the trip.

And yet… yes, I have a caveat. I loved the course. I am hugely impressed at what has been created in turning a derelict old military base with contaminated land into a magnificent top-class golf course which carefully respects its local environment. I was lucky to play it on a warm and sunny August evening with that lovely links light you get at that time of day. My caveat is heavily influenced by comparison with my next visit in the following chapter to another links course on an island in Denmark. While Budersand is immeasurably the better course, somehow the experience wasn't quite as heart-warming. Perhaps it was the lack of a characterful clubhouse; perhaps it was the somewhat utilitarian looking buildings, including the hotel, which neighbour the course in certain places; perhaps it was the knowledge that this was a 10-year-old course as opposed to a 100-year-old one; perhaps it was just the way I felt that day. When you read the next chapter you might understand a little more. But whatever, don't let my somewhat illogical and mainly emotional response dissuade you from visiting this modern masterpiece.

We enjoyed a good pub supper in the small town of Hornum before heading back to Westerland where we were staying.

In August the island is very busy as it is a favoured holiday destination for Germans from the northern cities. This 'busyness', however, is relative and we met little traffic when we took the one road north from Westerland to the small port of List which is situated at the northern end if not quite the northern tip of the island. This is about a twenty-minute drive, a little less than the trip to Budersand in the south. From Sylt we were to take the early morning ferry over to the neighbouring Danish island of Rømø – but before doing that I had another mission.

I mentioned at the Slyrs distillery that there was a connection with Sylt. In List's small harbour is a boat called *The Angel's Share* and on this boat Slyrs distillery is maturing some of its spirit. It believes that maturing it in this seaside atmosphere will give it very particular characteristics, perhaps a bit like some of the island Scottish malts. I like this experimentation: maturation 1500 metres up a mountain or floating in a harbour in the North Sea. There is another 'Sylt' or 'Sild' edition maturing in an underground bunker on the island. As my whisky adventure progresses, I see this experimentation in maturation as central to the diversity of products being produced – in Scandanavia we will also see some more eccentric experiments. What difference does it make? I don't know. Maybe it's all in the story, but that's no bad thing.

The charming thatched clubhouse at Fanø Links

The dunes at Fanø Links are so natural you can't tell that there is a golf course within them

CHAPTER SEVEN

DENMARK

'I have found golf to be a universal language wherever I have travelled at home or abroad.'

Ben Hogan (1912-1997)

American professional golfer; winner of nine major championships

THE FERRY CROSSING from Sylt to Denmark is to the Danish island of Rømø which you cross and then drive over a causeway to the mainland. Rømø has a sleepy feel to it being much less busy than Sylt. From the mainland there is about a half hour's drive up to the port of Esbjerg from where you take another ferry to reach the small island of Fanø.

It only takes about 15 minutes to the small town of Havneby on Fanø. Fanø is a smaller, quieter and quainter version of Sylt. That is both its strength and its weakness. Like all small, fairly remote islands, its lack of scale in terms of population and visitors gives it charm but is economically challenging. I found this on the Uist islands in Scotland – they are that much more remote and therefore quieter than, for example, Skye and so it is much more difficult to sustain quality accommodation and restaurants. It is a delicate balance but Fanø is undeniably very scenic from its extensive beaches, pretty countryside, incredible wildlife and small charming towns. The most obviously charming is Sønderho on the southern tip with its narrow streets of thatched cottages – it is regularly voted Denmark's prettiest village. It also has some good restaurants.

While it was golf that prompted my visit, it is probably the birdlife which attracts the most visitors. The Wadden Sea, which surrounds Fanø, is one of the world's largest tidal areas – it extends off the coasts of The Netherlands and Germany as well as Denmark – and is a UNESCO World Heritage Site. The shallow waters are home to some 10,000 species and during the course of a year over 10 million birds roost there. What is remarkable about the area is that with the tides, storm surges and wind, the landscape is constantly changing as enormous quantities of sand are being moved on an almost daily basis. As well as sand dunes being eroded, new ones are being created so the shape of the island of Fanø is always changing. Sønderho some 200 years ago looked out over a wide bay and had a harbour; today it looks out over miles of marshes and mudflats as the sea has deposited large quantities of sand. As a result, the island is much more a magnet for ecologists and birdwatchers than golfers.

At time of writing, Denmark has just one player in the men's top 100 world ranked golfers and two in the women's. The Hojgaard twins achieved the remarkable feat of winning on consecutive weeks on the European Tour in 2021. Perhaps the most famous Danish golfer is Thomas Bjørn who until recently was famed for being one of many golfers who 'nearly won The Open'. It was at Royal St George's in 2003 when in the last round he stood on the 16th tee with a two-shot lead. What followed, while not quite akin to Jean van de Velde at Carnoustie two years earlier, was a golfing calamity. His ball narrowly missed the green and rolled into a deep bunker from where he took three shots to get out. What many people forget is that he had had further bunker trouble in the first round when he had been penalised two shots on the 17th for hitting the sand with his club after another failed bunker shot – under the recent law changes this transgression is no longer a penalty. Happily, many now remember Thomas as the triumphant European Team Captain at the Ryder Cup held in Paris in 2018.Many of Denmark's top courses have been built in the past two decades, often to American style designs. As throughout Europe, a market has been established for these new resort-style courses. I have nothing against them and I am sure that I would enjoy some of them but I generally feel that they lack charm. However, they are a necessary and important part of the development of the game; if golf is to develop in Denmark then 'championship' courses will need to be built which can hold professional tournaments. What it demonstrates is that there is an increasing gap between these requirements and what a regular mid-handicap golfer will enjoy. Many new course designs try to get round this by having an extensive range of tees to give courses different lengths and this often works to good effect. There is sometimes though an obsession with wanting to play off the back tees, to play the 'full course as it was intended'. This is nonsense. A good course can be just as testing and often much more enjoyable for a mid-handicap golfer when played to a yardage of say 6,000 yards rather than 7,000 yards. As we will see, Fanø is an excellent example of this.

It is interesting to read that the issue of the increasing distances the ball is being hit and the effect it is having on golf-course design has been around for nearly a century. We know that the R&A are considering what to do about it but this is not new. Robert Hunter, in his seminal work, *The Links,* published in 1926, devotes several pages to what he regards as the scourge of ball manufacturers 'adding length to the ball'. He makes the case for shorter courses, citing North Berwick which he states most golfers would rather play than 'on many long, tireless, featureless courses with a thousand more yards'. He concludes that 'some regulation of the golf ball is bound to come as a matter of common sense'. We will see.

While wildlife is Fanø's biggest claim to fame, it also has a remarkable golfing history. It has the oldest golf course in Denmark and the oldest proper links course in continental Europe. In the 1890s, Fanø became a popular seaside summer resort attracting members of European high society for spa holidays at its grand hotels. An old postcard advertises a ferry crossing from Harwich to Esbjerg, so clearly British high society was also attracted. The course was originally built in 1898 for a German wine merchant by a Scot, Robert Dunlop from Prestwick, and held the inaugural Danish Open in 1901 which was won by Dunlop himself. Dunlop, like many Scottish golfers, was to emigrate to the United States where sadly he apparently died tragically, falling into a frozen lake in 1907. The course was extended to 18 holes by a local engineer in 1930 but was then lost during the German occupation of the Second World War. The current club – Fanø Vesterhavsbad Golf Club – was formed in 1948. As recently as 2001, the course's centenary year, a number of substantial changes were made to the 1930 layout including some new holes, though playing the course you would not recognise them as new.

It is important to manage expectations. I could quickly suggest many reasons why you might not want to play at Fanø.

The course is very short by modern standards, only about 5,500 yards. There are many very short Par 4s. There are no bunkers. The condition of the course is not that good and all the teeing areas are raised mats. Some of the greens, most of which are quite small, have bumpy patches on them. The clubhouse is small and functional. So, you are not going to add this to your bucket list? Well, you are missing out. My round at Fanø was one of my most delightful golfing experiences I have ever had. This is the epitome of 'raw golf', how golf evolved and how golf is best played. The course is built on pure links land, a low-lying dunescape with native lyme grasses and heather. There are no trees. Its look is wonderfully understated. Indeed, it is so natural looking that often the golf course is not evident. It is a totally natural environment for fauna and flora. And here the contrast with Budersand can be understood; Fanø feels like a 100+ year old course whereas Budersand, despite the natural look which has been created, feels like a new course. While Budersand was a beautiful environment some of the surrounding buildings did not add to the experience whereas at Fanø the buildings you can see are mainly thatched Friesian cottages.

But it is not all about the ambience and the environment because the course also has proper golfing credentials. Each tee shot requires thought. Driver, 3-wood or iron are nearly always options as you need to be thinking about what shot you will be playing next. The layout is such that the wind direction changes constantly and sometimes subtly. There are a lot of short Par 4s but there are many different ways of playing these holes; long drives to get as near as possible will not always deliver the easiest second shot. There are often small ridges crossing the fairways at tricky angles; you have to think carefully all the time. There are a number of blind shots so the golfing experience does benefit from playing it more than once. It is, however, the ultimate links experience, a classic example of the running game and Fine Golf's 'joy to be alive' feeling.

A few holes deserve specific mention. Take the 5th, here the comparison is with the famous 'Dell' hole at Lahinch in Ireland, a blind Par 3 into a gathering green. It is, I suppose, possible that Dunlop had played at Lahinch as it had been laid out a few years before. I was amazed to read afterwards that the 9th hole was new, being part of the 2001 changes. It is a short Par 4, very much in the style of many of Dunlop's original holes with a raised tee giving a view of a number of landing areas on a bumpy fairway. Where best to approach the green from? A green which you can see from the tee but which will be hidden when you play your second. The only Par 5 on the back 9 is the 11th which wends its way through the low-lying dunes ending with a tricky third shot over some heather to a small green. It's a Par 5, so the small green works well. And finally, there is the 17th with its hogsback fairway which requires accuracy off the tee to deliver the best approach to a very narrow green nestling beneath the dunes. And since I played, there is a bit of good news which is likely to make the golfing experience even richer: in 2022 the club took over the lease on its land, appointed a full-time greenkeeper and has gained a grant to invest in new, environmentally friendly machinery to restore the quality of the course.

Serendipity? Happenstance? I'm not sure which is the right word (they are both, what I would call, 'good words') for a coincidence that seems too extraordinary. There I was on an island off the west coast of Denmark, researching a book on whisky and golf. We had planned to play golf at about two o'clock but had been delayed as we had decided to have a quick lunch and it took us longer than expected to pay for it because the restaurant's card machine had broken down. So, there were various factors which caused us to be preparing to tee off when we did. But as it happened, we were teeing off just as two gentlemen were coming off the 18th green. One was clad not just in traditional plus-fours but tartan ones to boot. I also noticed a Prestwick logo on his shirt so naturally went up and introduced myself. Mikael was a delightful local member who then introduced me to his friend, Niels. I explained why I was visiting Fanø and that I was writing a book about whisky and golf. At this point, he reached into his golf bag and produced a bottle of malt whisky! A bottle taken from his own barrel matured at Bruichladdich on Islay. It transpired that Mikael was a member of an august group called 'The Right Honourable Gentlemen Golfers' Whisky Association of March 19th 2003'. He never explained what happened on 19th March 2003 but I wish I had been there. Indeed, he was no less than 'Chieftain' of this splendid organisation explaining how they toured Scotland every year to experience what they regarded as the best links courses in the world as well as a few whiskies.

You probably think that I am making this up but I am not. They even have a website which records their adventures over the years including video footage of their various exploits. Some of it is positively cinematic. Mikael explained that Niels was their 'webmaster' as well as being 'Deputy Chieftain'. There is much to say about this. The coincidence of meeting Mikael and Niels was positively serendipitous but actually it confirms how golf and whisky provide a common language and can be such positive forces for long established friendships and how the values of competitive links golf transcend nationalities and cultures. There is also a strong respect for the game's history and a love of Scotland which is not only felt by Scots like me but by people all over the world. Their course at Fanø had been originally designed by a man from Prestwick and they wanted to find out about Prestwick and they liked what they saw. The inspiration behind many of the start-up whisky distilleries in Europe, including the one in Denmark which we are about to visit, happened in the same way.

He insisted that we try a dram of his malt – Niels was despatched into the clubhouse to get glasses – which was an excellent start to our round. Mikael was incredibly proud of Fanø and rightly so. He has on his trips played all the top Open courses so has experienced the great links courses but knows that in Fanø he has a little gem of a course in the most beautiful surroundings which delivers a truly authentic links experience. Further mention must be made of the clubhouse. This is a small but attractive building. Paying for the golf was via an 'honesty box', something which is quite familiar in Scotland, but it was the first golf clubhouse which I have been to which also operated an 'honesty bar'. Magnificent. I can't wait to go back.

After taking the ferry back onto the mainland it is worth noting that Esbjerg has one of Denmark's best-known golf clubs. It boasts 42 holes (two 18s and a 6 hole Par 3 course) and is situated in woodlands just to the north west of what is otherwise a mainly industrial port town. Our destination, the Fary Lochan Distillery, is about an hour's drive into central Jutland in the village of Farre just outside the small rural town of Give. While it feels quite remote it is in fact only twenty minutes from Billund Airport which has flights to the UK so Fanø Golf Club and Fary

Lochan Distillery could be accommodated on a long weekend trip from the UK. The scenery on the way through central Jutland is rural but it can't be called spectacular. Denmark is very flat. In fact, the highest mountain in Denmark is a gentle mound called Møllehøj (Mill Top) which rises to a mighty 561 feet. Views in Denmark are therefore few and far between.

Rather like its top golf courses, most of the whisky distilleries in Denmark have sprung up since the millennium. The first, and best known, was Stauning, started by a group of nine Scotch-loving friends in 2006. Their idea was to use traditional methods such as floor maltings, peat-fired kilns and direct-fired stills. They converted an old abattoir and began distilling on a small scale using specially designed pot stills sourced from Spain. By 2009 they had moved into nearby farm buildings and were developing a strong reputation. This was confirmed some six years later when they signed a contract with Distill Ventures, an investment arm of Diageo, which included a £10 million investment in capacity taking it to 900,000 litres. The plan is to stay true to their roots of using traditional production methods – there will be 24 direct-fired stills to produce this volume.

What the success of Stauning did was encourage other distillery start-ups across Denmark, some of which emerged from existing breweries where Denmark has an established reputation – Braunstein, just south of Copenhagen is a good example.

Fary Lochan's roots are similar to those of Stauning. The distillery was the brainchild of Jens-Erik Jorgensen who had visited Scotland and wanted to create a Danish equivalent of Scottish malts. He was inspired by the flavour of smoked cheeses his mother had served him as a child on the central Danish island of Fyn, which used nettle smoke, and he saw this as a way of producing Danish malts with a unique twist. He distilled his first product in 2009.There is, however, great sadness in the story. Jens-Erik contracted cancer and died suddenly in 2014. By this time the distillery was well established and his widow and their three sons now run the business which has grown successfully.

The distinctive small pot still at Fary Lochan Distillery

I always talk about the importance of location for both golf courses and whisky distilleries and Fary Lochan is no exception. Farre is a sleepy little agricultural village. While the flat countryside cannot be said to have any particular scenic merit, the distillery itself is set in a very peaceful location on the edge of a forest. And this location *is* relevant as it is from this forest that the nettles are picked which give Fary Lochan its distinctiveness. The distillery site is a complex of small buildings designed to complement the woodland setting. There are a few small lakes and it was only when visiting that I understood that 'Lochan' in the distillery name is of course the Scots word for small lochs or lakes. This is a working distillery but the environment has a strongly artisan feel. Production is not fully automated with different parts of the process being undertaken in different buildings. The stills are familiar pot stills sourced from Scotland and the hand-picked nettles are burnt in a small smoke oven outside. Indeed, the biggest building with the most spacious room is reserved for meetings as the business has 375 shareholders who are all invited regularly to review progress of the venture. In the middle of this room is a small spiral staircase which leads up to a small roof top 'hide' which looks out over the forest. Jens-Erik and his wife used to spend time up there contemplating their vision and to this day the management use it to gather together with a dram to muse on their next steps. The other main space is for the maturation of the spirit in barrels and this is done underground in a smart dungeon-like space which recreates proper dunnage warehouse conditions. Again, this has been done, as with everything at Fary Lochan, with a degree of flair and style.

The business now also produces gins, fruit liqueurs and schnapps which add to the product range and help generate cash. The focus, however, is unashamedly whisky. I bought a bottle to take home which was expensive, some €70 for a 50cl bottle. I am not sure to what extent that is premium pricing or tax. It was 54% alcohol so nearly cask strength, there was no age statement so I am guessing it was quite young. Apart from a batch number

'Winter 02', there is no further detail on the expression beyond generic statements about the artisanal and traditional approach to making whisky. Even I, very much an amateur taster, would have liked some hint as to how it had been matured. I have to say it was not my favourite whisky when I took it home to taste – I gave it several attempts – but I have read several very positive reviews of their various products since, so I urge you to pay very little attention to my still poorly educated palate. It is clearly a business that knows what it is doing and the nettle smoking is producing a distinctive product.

The subtleties of malt whisky tasting have made me wonder whether Covid could be a threat to some experts. It has been widely reported that Covid has impacted some people's sense of taste and smell. There were reports of wine sommeliers being unable to do their job properly. What about whisky master blenders? If Covid did affect some people's taste in the long term, is it possible to detect this? Might there be an imperceptible change in the taste delivery of some major whiskies as a result of Covid? We will never know.

The pretty clubhouse at Falsterbo has a very relaxed feel

The attractive grounds of the hotel at The Spirit of Hven Distillery

CHAPTER EIGHT

SWEDEN

'Good whisky, as a beverage, is the most wholesome spirit in the world'

Alfred Barnard (1837-1918)

Historian and whisky author

FROM FARY LOCHAN it is about a three-hour drive to Copenhagen, the Danish capital, which, it is easy to forget, is situated on its own island at the very eastern end of Denmark. You join the E20, the main motorway which stretches across the whole country from Copenhagen to Esbjerg, just short of the prettily located Fredericia, from where you cross a high bridge onto Denmark's central island, Fyn. This takes you past the second city of Odense and then across another impressive, long bridge at Nyborg onto Zeeland. We are headed past the south end of Copenhagen, beyond the airport where we will take the bridge across the Straights of Øresund into Sweden. There is much to say about this bridge which came to prominence with the famous television Swedish crime series 'The Bridge'. At 8 kms, it is the longest combined road and rail bridge in Europe (the longest is the Vasco de Gama bridge in Lisbon which is double the length). However, there are also 4 kms of tunnel to get you across the straights and it is an exciting ride whether by car or train. Understandably it is a toll bridge but I have to say that I was not prepared for the toll charge which was an eye-watering €60, whether you pay in Danish or Swedish Krona. It takes time to adjust as Swedish and Danish Krona are now quite different in value. Having carefully budgeted my trip I was caught out by spending over £100 to cross the bridge and back.

Once I had recovered from this shock it was just a short drive south down the coast to the small holiday resort of Falsterbo which is situated on a narrow peninsula on Sweden's most south-westerly tip, where the Øresund Straights meet the Baltic Sea. Falsterbo was a rich town in the Middle Ages as a centre for the lucrative herring-fishing market and enjoyed trading privileges as part of the Hanseatic League. Today it is mainly a holiday destination for Swedes from Stockholm and the north of the country who come to enjoy its more temperate climate. It is a small sleepy town. I remember arriving at our accommodation and asking for directions to the town centre so that we could look for somewhere to eat. This elicited a puzzled response because there is really no 'town centre', just numerous quiet residential streets. We were encouraged to go down to the harbour where there were a few fish restaurants. Rather like Fanø, it is also a magnificent place for migrating sea birds which populate the expansive sandflats.

The golf club was founded in 1909 making it one of the oldest in Sweden. It is situated on the most southerly point of the peninsula though initially the first 9 holes were built a little to the east until it was established that the quality of grass was not good enough. In 1911 fresh land was leased around the lighthouse and a new 9 holes laid out. It became 18 holes in the early 1930s and it is fundamentally this layout which survives today though considerable work was undertaken in the 1990s to the greens, tees and bunker positions.Before talking about the course, I would like to mention the clubhouse and the 'club' generally. Very seldom have I arrived at a golf club as a visitor and felt so welcome and so at home. I immediately felt that this was a club I would enjoy being a member of. The first thing to note is that the car park had relatively few cars in it but the bicycle park was full. Most members seem to cycle to Falsterbo. The clubhouse is a charming wooden construction which faces two ways: onto a large putting green as you approach it and out onto the course where it actually overlooks the 7th green. The putting green and surrounds which include a large practice area were a buzz of activity when we visited on a Monday morning in August and what was noticeable was the vast spread of ages. Unaffectedly, there were 8-year-olds and 80-year-olds sharing the putting green and what looked like a fairly even mix of sexes. It had a genuine family feel to it. I was travelling with my colleague from Beaconsfield and we were put in a four-ball with two members, Lars and Johann, both of whom were in Falsterbo for their holidays. There is always a degree of nervousness when this happens. Would we be seen as a bit of a distraction from their game – they were handing in their cards – and would they really welcome us as golfing companions? From very early on, it was clear that they were perfectly happy to be joined by two strange Brits and by the end of the round we were enjoying healthy banter. We were all of a similar handicap – presumably the club had thought this through – and we all had our ups and downs. It was as if we had been playing together for years. Such is the common language that is golf.

There are two distinct areas of the course; most of it is a classic links on relatively flat land but there are about six holes (2-6 and the short 11th) which are of a different character as they are routed amongst water with high reeds. In theory it is also links – the turf is the same – but in practice it has a different feel to it as it is more like playing around modern-style water hazards. The course begins by heading north and into the reed area for a loop of six holes before returning to the clubhouse for the 7th, a short Par 4 where an accurate tee shot is required. The course then heads back out and routes around the old lighthouse. Many will mention the short Par 3 11th as it is an attractive hole across water with the distinctive wooden bridge to get to the green. In truth, it is not a typical links hole and the main challenge is judging the distance in the wind which is nearly always a factor at Falsterbo. There is another Par 3 at 14 which is a tough 200 yard plus, in front of the lighthouse. Probably the best stretch is the final four: 15 is a long straight Par 5 with a trickily situated pond short of the green; 16 is a sweeping Par 4 to a slightly uphill green in the corner of the bird sanctuary; the 17th tee is a beautiful spot – Lars said it was his favourite place on earth – as you look out towards the dunes and the thousands of seabirds and then turn back to see the entirety of the links and the clubhouse in the distance; 17, a dog-leg Par 4, starts the journey back; 18 is another Par 5 which makes its way back to the delightful clubhouse with the course to the left and the dunes and beach to the right. As it is often played with the prevailing westerly wind, this Par 5 will be reachable in two for many golfers but the second shot will need to be accurate as the green is tricky.

Fortunately, we had time for a beer on the delightful veranda overlooking the course. The clubhouse has a homely feel with a number of different rooms, a fireplace and armchairs. The food looked excellent and the restaurant was doing a good trade the day we visited. It all adds to the club feel and it is clear that Falsterbo has an affinity with the traditions of the game. Golf has a long tradition in Sweden but it has also boomed in the past 30 years. The first Swede to play in The Ryder Cup was Joakim Haeggman in 1993 and Swedes have been regular features in the European team since – indeed in 2002 there were three Swedes in the team. (I bet you can't name them.) Henrik Stenson's memorable victory in The Open at Troon in 2016 was the first by a Swede, but over twenty years earlier Jesper Parnevik was only a shot behind Nick Price after a memorable battle at Turnberry in 1994. Of course, in women's golf, Anneka Sörenstam can lay claim to being one of the all-time greats.

The Swedes are also great fans of hickory golf which is becoming increasingly popular. Falsterbo hosted a 'Hickory Ryder Cup' in 2009. What I find remarkable playing with hickory clubs is the skill required to play with them. Hickory golf really is the antidote to the modern big hitters where the ability to hit the ball enormous distances confers such an advantage. Golf with hickory clubs is in many ways much more skilful; it is remarkable to note the scores achieved by the likes of Harry Vardon and his contemporaries without modern equipment with their large sweet spots and stiff shafts. Steel shafts weren't allowed until 1924 (initially for putters only) by the USGA and later by the R&A. Cyril Thomas used a steel shafted putter in his surprise 1924 US Open victory but the first major to be won using all steel shafts was Billy Burke at the US Open in 1931. It is likely that hickory golf will grow in the coming years with the renewed interest in 'running game' golf and links-style bumpy courses and it will be members of courses and clubs like Falsterbo who will embrace it. It is certainly something I intend to play more of as I think it will help my understanding of how golf developed. Falsterbo really is a little bit of Scottish golfing tradition.

Sweden is also beginning to develop a whisky tradition. The Swedes have been great afficionados of Single Malt Scotch Whisky for some time. Recently a Single Malt Fund has been launched on the Nordic Growth Market exchange in Stockholm. And over the past 20 years the country has become an increasingly enthusiastic producer. Perhaps the best-known brand is Mackmyra which is now available in mainstream UK retail outlets. Mackmyra has also become known as a business using innovation to develop its product range by using Artificial Intelligence to identify successful recipes. This caused some initial disbelief amongst whisky traditionalists but what Mackmyra was really doing was recognising that there are an infinite number of variables involved in making a great malt whisky and seeking to narrow down the successful elements for their master blender to approve. Swedish scientists have also been involved in researching the effect of adding water to whisky and how it releases aromatic compounds which can enhance the aroma and therefore the flavour. Sweden deserves a special place in any discussion of how whisky is developing across the world.

The two most famous distilleries, Mackmyra and Box, are situated in the north of the country where, understandably, the golf courses are less prevalent. There are also a number of distilleries situated on the Baltic islands such as Gotland, Øland and Bornholm but we are headed to another island situated in the Straights of Øresund just north of Malmö. You can reach it by ferry from Copenhagen but the quickest journey is from

Landskrona about 30 miles north of Malmö and less than an hour's drive from Falsterbo. On the way you will pass a more famous Swedish golf course, Barsebäck, which has held many Scandanavian Masters events as well as The Solheim Cup in 2003.

Landskrona is an attractive medieval town with some fine old buildings, a museum and art galleries. It is also the ferry port for the island of Hven or Ven –I'm still not quite sure how it is spelt. This is probably because of Hven's history (I will stick with Hven as this is what the distillery is called) which, rather like Berwick-upon-Tweed, has been fought over across the centuries and at various times been part of both Denmark and Sweden. It was invaded by the Vikings, Peter 1st of Russia and Napoleon so has had a torrid history because of its strategic location. It is situated in the middle of the Straights of Øresund, possibly slightly nearer the Swedish side, and is no more than 5 kms from north to south and about 2 kms from west to east. It has approximately 350 inhabitants. Yes, it is quite small!

It is also very peaceful with very few cars (it promotes cycling holidays) and consists of pleasant, though unspectacular, gentle countryside. Its most famous historical citizen was probably Tycho Brahe, the 16th century Danish astronomer who started developing many of the astronomical theories of Copernicus – there is a small museum dedicated to Brahe in the middle of the island.

The ferry journey from Landskrona takes only about 45 minutes and you arrive at the small ferry terminal at Backvicken. You do not need to plan your travel on the island because all ferries are met by the Venbussen (yes, Hven genuinely has 'an integrated transport system') which will take you wherever you need on the island. It has a set route but special requests are catered for and, despite the language barrier, we managed to get a small detour to take us directly to the distillery.

The Spirit of Hven is more than just a distillery. It is also a hotel and conference centre and has a bar and an exceptionally good restaurant. The business is run by Henric and Anja Molin and before going into detail I will start by simply saying it is wonderful.

Henric is a chemist by trade but also a whisky enthusiast and it is the marrying of this skill with this passion that has created such a distinctive business. Henric understands the detail of the distilling process and is keen to experiment in all sorts of ways. The distillery produces a wide range of spirits but whisky, and the mystery of how it is made, is his core interest. In order to experiment the distillery seems to have all processes covered. He has a large, brand-new, stainless-steel column still which has been made to his own design. He has also built himself a replica of an old 19th century Coffey still made of wood – it is a startlingly good-looking piece of kit. And, of course, he also has pot stills.

Henric has also developed an internationally recognised laboratory and consultancy business where he does analytical work for distillers all around the world including the big multi-nationals. I get the sense that this is an important business stream and it allows him to experiment with his own products. His product range is broad but, being organic and 'super-premium', the volumes are relatively small. The tour I was given was unlike any other distillery tour with Henric being keen not only to show off his distilling kit but also his state-of-the-art scientific analytical instruments.

Apart from the experimental approach to the actual distilling with the combinations of a column still, the Coffey still and the copper pot stills, Henric also likes to experiment with maturation. Oak is his favoured wood but he talked about the different properties of oaks from different parts of the world. He is also maturing spirits other than whisky such as his gin, vodka, Swedish aquavit and winter and summer spirits. Traditionally whisky's maturation is what differentiates it from other spirits – remember in some countries 'whisky or whiskey' can be distilled from other raw materials such as molasses in India. Then again, Henric sees a role for limited maturation, generally in virgin oak casks, for these other spirits to give them depth of character. We tasted a particularly rich matured rum.

There was one other maturation experiment which has to be mentioned; I still don't know whether this one was genuine or a gimmick. As you walk through the distillery you come across a rack of barrels maturing in oak all 'wearing' headphones – yes, headphones. And each barrel is labelled with a different style of music from 'rock' and 'reggae' to 'blues' and 'Vivaldi'. Henric insists that the different vibrations made by these different genres of music will inevitably affect the style of whisky. I suppose that I can understand how different music will produce perhaps subtle movements within the maturing barrel. But will this really affect the taste? Or the mouthfeel? Or is this Henric just having a bit of fun? Is it just a bit of a wind-up? Genuinely, I don't know!

I do believe, however, that music can also have an impact on your enjoyment of tasting the product; a whisky, I would suggest is best enjoyed with gentle and calming music – more Vivaldi than rock. Maybe this is my prejudice. But, as I have said before, the context is important. I was amused to read recently that this theory has been backed up by an experiment undertaken by a Californian wine merchant. He tested the same champagne in five different glasses amongst a number of people. The glass tasted in silence was the least preferred; the glass tasted to the accompaniment of the third movement of the Brahms Violin Concerto was unanimously voted the best. As the tempo and expression for this piece is described as 'Allegro giocoso' (fast and cheerful) this makes a lot of sense.

Yes, these barrels of maturing whisky at Hven really are enjoying listening to different genres of music – will 'Reggae' or 'Vivaldi' produce the smoother taste?

If the scientific laboratory is an important business stream so too is the hotel, restaurant and conference centre which is run by Anja. I can only say that we were royally looked after. The quality of the food and the standard of the service was first class. The accommodation in small wooden cottages was spacious and clean and the meal was excellent. We were also given a tasting of the full range of products before dinner. This involved not just the whiskies but also the gin, vodka and aquavit. I am not a gin expert but it was deliciously smooth and could easily be drunk neat. I have since noticed that it has had many good reviews on various gin-tasting websites and it is apparently the only gin served at Noma in Copenhagen, often regarded as the world's best restaurant. I can only say that I enjoyed this extensive tasting which was then followed by some seriously good wines with dinner. Despite all this my head was totally clear the following morning. My theory on this is simple: the higher quality the spirit – and I think Henric's spirit is very high quality – the less you will suffer any after effects of a little too much indulgence. To be clear however, my indulgence was, of course, purely in the interests of research.

Focusing on the whisky, again the range is broad, reflecting Henric's interest in experimentation which covers mash ingredients, yeasts and the use of different oaks in maturation. As well as many different malt whiskies there are corn and rye whiskies. While the first whisky was released in 2012 (distilling had begun in 2008) the first core expression was not made until 2015. It is called Tyco's Star but even this is a complex product made with a mix of three malts: pale ale malt, chocolate malt and a heavily peated whisky malt. Maturation is then in three different types of oak from Missouri, south-western France and the Bourgogne. The other main malts make up the 'Seven Stars' range, each one named after a star from Ursa Major as a tribute to Tyco Brahe and each comprising a different mix of barleys and a different maturation regime. An analysis of all these could be a subject for a book in its own right. Forgive the slightly strained comparison, but Henric's whisky is the equivalent of bump and run golf – he has a pick and mix approach to producing different products and, just as in links golf, there are many ways of making a good shot. He has no fixed method because he recognises that a fixed method would be boring. So too with 'target' golf courses where a mechanical swing will hit the ball an exact distance and the ball stop to order. It doesn't lend itself to excitement.

What was a disappointment was that I was unable to buy any of Henric's whisky. Swedish legislation is such that retail purchases are only allowed in government stores. The only option was to drink in the bar or pay for the contents of the Mini Bar (which I did).

New distillery businesses come in many different forms. Some look to focus on whisky while others take advantage of the obvious synergies by producing other spirits. For some, the 'visitor centre' and shop are a central part of the business. This can depend on the location. The Spirit of Hven is unique in many ways and very much reflective of its owners, Henric and Anja. The location restricts the potential number of visitors so they rely on maximising the experience for those who do make it to the island. It is an idyllic, peaceful spot so the hotel and conference centre are a great asset. And Henric's laboratory allows him both to leverage his skill and to embark on a range of experiments with his product range.

Finally, I must mention the 'ambience'. Start-up distilleries are generally friendly places but there was an air of welcome about everything at Backafallen. There are whisky distilleries which I am pleased to have visited – this is one where I really want to return.

The Arctic beauty and peacefulness of the island of Myken

There is always a dramatic view wherever you look at Lofoten Links

CHAPTER NINE

NORWAY

'There are no shortcuts to any place worth going'

Beverley Sills (1929-2007)

American Soprano

GOOGLE MAPS TELLS me that it is a 49-hour drive from Granada in Spain to Bodo in Norway which will be the central base for this final chapter. 4,743 kilometres or just under 3,000 miles. Amusingly the recommended route takes you past the Owl Distillery in Liege featured in Chapter 3 and across the Oresund Bridge so you will get a view of Falsterbo from a distance and drive past Landskrona from where I got the ferry to Hven in Chapter 8. However, there are quicker ways to get to Bodo. I was planning to fly to Trondheim, a pretty university town, whence you can either take a scenic ten-hour train journey or a short flight. Covid 19 meant that my flight was cancelled and I had to go via Oslo. Bodo is about 50 miles inside the Arctic Circle and is in itself a rather unremarkable town though it has a pleasant marina. The reason for visiting is that from here you can get ferries both to the island of Myken, a little further south, and to the Lofoten Islands to the north which are respectively the locations of our final whisky distillery and golf course visits.

Norwegian ferry timetables take a little getting used to. In Scotland, with Caledonian McBrayne pretty much the sole operator, it is usually easier to find out what is possible. Norway is a little more complicated and the ferries, especially to remote islands like Myken, only operate on certain days and are very seasonal. They are, however, impressive. I will in this chapter make many comparisons between Norway and Scotland and the provision of ferries is one. The survival of communities on many of the islands is totally dependant on ferries which clearly also have to be state-subsidised. Providing long term security to island communities by investing in the infrastructure for providing a quality ferry service, both for maintaining day to day existence and to encourage tourism (which in turn bolsters the economy of these places), seems to me exactly the sort of thing a devolved Scottish government should prioritise. The well-publicised problems with the Scottish government's investment in new ferries can, at very least, be described as 'disappointing'. The ferry to Myken was a brand new 'fast boat', certainly a more modern and impressive vessel than anything I have experienced on dear old Calmac in Scotland. The journey was about three hours and included several stops at other small islands which dominate the coastline. Myken is the most remote of these islands, sitting outside the main archipelagos, some 20 miles off the coast just inside the Arctic Circle.

It was on this ferry, or 'fast boat', that I met my first Myken inhabitant. The boat had a capacity of 147 passengers (no cars) but there were less than a dozen of us and I think I stood out. Petter-Inge Petterson soon engaged me in conversation. He said that I looked like a professor or perhaps a government inspector and if I were the latter, he would have phoned ahead to warn the distillery!

It soon became clear that Myken (pronounced *mick-en*) is not just an island but a community. In winter, it is a very small community with just 12 inhabitants. In summer, it grows a bit but is still just two figures. Petter-Inge's wife's family come from the island and they are renovating a house which they will live in during the summer months. Petter-Inge worked in the fishing industry, Norway's third largest export sector after oil and gas and metals. Indeed, fishing is an industry that has sustained many of the small communities on remote islands and in distant areas of Norway and is relevant to the story of the Myken distillery which I will explain later. In the meantime, Petter-Inge enthusiastically pointed out each of the many islands we were passing and how the shapes of these volcanic creations resembled different animals: one like a giant sitting lion, another a shark's fin and another a caped horseman. It required a little imagination but reminded me of a game I played with my children looking for shapes of animals in the clouds. As we pushed out further into the ocean, there were fewer islands and the weather cleared – often the clouds hug the coastline while further out to sea, Myken enjoys clear sunshine. Unlike the tall rocks of the islands we had passed, Myken has a flatter, gentler look, more Islay than Jura. As we approached the small jetty, Petter-Inge pointed out his house and the distillery which was next to the landing area. I was met not only by Roar Larsen from the distillery but also the owner of the Myken apartments where I was staying – a ferry arrival is an event in Myken. Roar greeted me and said that a tour had been arranged for 4 o'clock and suggested that he booked me in for dinner at the only restaurant on the island afterwards. My apartment (next door to the distillery) was not quite ready yet so Petter-Inge suggested that I leave my bags outside (I might have looked cautious at this suggestion as he immediately laughed and said that nobody was likely to steal it on Myken) and accompany him and his wife to their home where he would cook me a lunch of eggs with bacon.

Myken has one 'street' which is apparently 850 metres long (the total island is about 2 kilometres long by 400 metres wide) with small houses along perhaps half of it. There are no cars and it is delightfully peaceful. I was only on the island about 24 hours but in that time was able to take two walks which encompassed everywhere you can walk. There are two small peaks which offer the best views and I was delighted to meet a young researcher who was doing his annual survey of house sparrows on the island. There was something magical and innocent about the place.

Before we got to Petter-Inge's house, we stopped at the shop (it opens daily from 11am to 2pm) for a coffee while he bought the eggs and bacon. Their current house is small but with a delightful view over the waterfront and they showed me the neighbouring building which they were renovating. The bacon omelette was hearty and welcome.

I am not sure what I expected but Myken is unlike anything else I have experienced. Perhaps Raasey in Scotland with its new distillery is similar yet Raasey is a short hop from Skye, not three hours on a fast boat. And the story is a touching one. In 2008 Roar and his wife Trude were sailing up the coast of Norway with their children and stopped off at Myken. They stayed a few days as the weather was not so good, loved it so much that the following year they returned and decided to stay. Roar, a Professor of Chemistry in Trondheim, working mainly in the oil and gas industry, gave up his job and looked to build a future for his family on the island. They wrote down on two sheets of paper a series of ideas of how they could make a living on the island as well as contributing to sustaining the island's future and a whisky distillery was the winning idea. How brave is that? The shareholders are six couples who all have links to the island. Four years later they bought a building on the waterfront which was a disused fish processing plant. The story demonstrates how whisky distilling has replaced fish processing to provide a sustainable future for the island; following the closure of the school, the permanent population of the island had fallen to just six but it is now on the increase. There remain serious challenges for the community. Last year a damaged cable meant that they lost power for six months and had to rely on a diesel generator which didn't contribute to the island's peaceful setting. They are now looking at how a hydrogen plant linked to the distillery can provide a sustainable long-term power solution.

But the good news is that the distillery is a success. Whisky (and gin) is being produced. Products are being sold and exported. Visitor numbers are increasing and the Myken name is becoming known in the whisky world. And that means that the community on the island will survive. This success lies behind Petter-Inge and his wife's decision to invest in the properties on the island of her birth. The lighthouse has been made into an eight-bedroomed rental property. An Icelander has invested in the Myken Apartments. The distillery is now running out of storage space and as I was there a warehouse (delightfully called 'The Whisky Cathedral') was being erected to store the precious spirit. This building is architecturally sympathetic to its surroundings and will become a feature on the island, and so it should as whisky is the new fish and will become central to the island's future. The decision to store it on the island where it will experience the island's distinctive climate is an important statement about the integrity of the product and the brand.

Somehow, I had expected 'Roar' to be a larger than life, a loud ebullient character. In fact, he is slight, mild-mannered and quietly spoken. He is clearly proud of what they have achieved but is not one to boast about it. I was shown around the distillery by his wife Trude who also has a real passion for their project and impressive knowledge about the product they produce plus plenty of ideas about how they can be distinctive. The distillery is very 'artisan' and during my visit there was no real production flow and the building was very crowded as the new 'whisky cathedral' warehouse had not yet been completed so all the spirit storage was still on site. The copper stills came from Spain and on my visit they were experimenting with a new 'square' stainless-steel mash tun. The product is 'the real thing' inspired by authentic Scottish malts; the malted barley comes from German and Belgian producers of pilsner malt (though they are looking to find barley from Norway) and they are experimenting with mixes of distillers' and brewers' yeasts. But what about the magic third ingredient, water? The provenance of the water source is often used in the marketing of many of the great Single Malt Scotch brands – think of the Tarlogie Springs at Glenmorangie or the Kinchie burn from the Lammermuir Hills at Glenkinchie – but here the island offers no water source so the water is from the Myken municipal desalination plant, which doesn't sound very romantic. Yes, it is desalinated water that is used throughout the process (though the water used for cooling is directly pumped seawater) and is used in reducing the ABV to its target level. I am not aware of anywhere else that does this – does it make a difference? I am not qualified to judge. Certainly, my understanding of the process suggests that the water is a very minor contributor to taste – after all, many Scottish distilleries which put spirit in casks at their distillery then bottle it in the central belt of Scotland where distilled water will be used to dilute it to the target ABV strength.

What everyone knows *does* make a difference is the casks used and here, as well as the conventional ex-Bourbon (Maker's Mark and Heaven Hill) and 50-litre Oloroso sherry casks, they are experimenting with virgin Hungarian oak and Pineau de Charente casks, neither of which I have come across before. I like this attempt to add some differentiation while sticking to a classic process.

Marketing whisky is a challenge in Norway because, as in Sweden, sales are controlled through a government monopoly and advertising is strictly controlled. Yet Myken's market will be whisky enthusiasts rather than a mass market, people like me who seek out new stories and distinctive new ventures. And when you have a story as distinctive as this, word of mouth will spread fast.

I had spent only one night and about 24 hours on the island but I felt as if I had been there for a long time and knew everyone there was to know. I had enjoyed a delightful dinner in the one restaurant which is located at the top of the distillery building and is run by the wife of the Chairman. Everyone, locals and visitors alike, sat down and ate together and we were treated to Petter-Inge leading a sing-song with his guitar. I then enjoyed a quiet drink afterwards with Roar hearing about his ambitions. At dinner it was said that they needed to bottle some stock of gin and if anyone was able to, they could turn up at the distillery the following morning at 10am to help out. My ferry was not until noon so along with a group of others, locals and tourists alike, we formed an amateur production line to bottle, top, label and put into cases a pallet of the summer gin. All hands to the pump, literally.

I don't think that I have ever felt so uplifted by the experience of visiting a start-up distillery. I admire all start-ups – the passion, the entrepreneurial flair, the persistence – but the story of Myken is somehow even more impressive and as I left on the noon ferry to return to Bodo I was in good heart.

It was an afternoon of two ferry journeys because as well as the three hours back to Bodo, I then had to catch another ferry for another three-hour journey to Moskenes at the western end of the Lofoten Islands in search of the nearest golf course to Myken. The Lofoten Islands are a large archipelago which extend outwards from the mainland in a south westerly direction. They are some 100 miles inside the Arctic Circle but remarkably only about two thirds of the way up Norway. Norway is enormous; if you were to fold it down from its most southerly point it would reach to Rome.

The Lofoten ferry was a large car ferry and by the time it had reached the small harbour at Moskenes at the southern end of the Lofoten Islands it was late evening and the weather was what in Scotland would be described as 'dreich'. My first view of the Lofoten Islands was the ghostly and, given their size, slightly threatening presence of large grey mountains which appeared through the mist as the ferry approached. As Lofoten Links was nearly a two hour drive up the islands from Moskenes, I had decided to stay for a couple of nights in Reine nearby so that I had time to explore. Reine is a small and quaintly picturesque fishing village nestled on a bay surrounded by large peaks. My hotel was made up of 'Rorbu' cabins, wooden fishing huts which are, along with high wooden structures used for hanging out fish to dry, a feature of the islands. The following morning, I climbed Reinebringen, a 450-metre peak which towers over Reine and affords the most magnificent views of the archipelago. The climb is extremely steep but the effort is well rewarded at the top.

The scenery of Lofoten reminds me of Scotland but with the dial turned up a few notches. The scale is that bit bigger; the mountains are taller, the expanses wider, the views longer yet there is a familiarity with, for example, the north-west highlands where the scenery is both grand and ever-changing. I had hired a car and the trip up through the spine of the islands (there is really only one main road) is spectacular. Indeed, the first half hour or so north from Reine is on an extraordinary road – I have driven along both Big Sur in California and the Great Ocean Road west of Melbourne in Australia but this matches both of these for the quality of scenery. It may be a long way to go to find a golf course but there is much to enjoy on the way. About halfway on my journey the road crosses to the northern side with a huge flat glacial valley (the area would make a good destination for a geography field-trip to study volcanic and glacial terrain) and in the distance you can see a large, distinctively shaped mountain sitting by itself on a large plain. This is the Hoven mountain which at 368 metres is not that high but its solitary presence dominates the landscape around. It sits on the island of Gimsoya which is where we are headed. It is not clear on Lofoten where one island ends and another starts as most are linked by bridges and causeways.

The Hoven mountain is the most obvious feature of Gimsoya as the immediate surrounding area is very flat but it is the coastline that is its other main attraction. And it is the geography of the coastline which offers the opportunity for us to complete this tour with what for me is the best experience for a golfer: a links course with sea views and a spectacular setting.

Lofoten Links dates back to 1991 when a local landowner, Tor Hov, started a golf club and contacted English architect Jeremy Turner to design some holes. Tor sadly died of cancer but his son Frode and Jeremy Turner were determined to complete the vision and initially six holes were laid out in 1998. These were then extended to nine in the early 2000s and then 18 in 2015 to produce the course we play today. The latest layout has been overseen by the current course manager, Jerry Mulvihill, who hails from Ballybunion so obviously knows a bit about great links golf courses. The development has been gradual and there remains much to do with financing for a clubhouse and hotel, which would help bring more visitors and generate more income to invest in the course, which is still proving elusive. It is a dilemma because Lofoten is very remote and justifying investment to bring in visitors is difficult, an extreme version of the challenge which has faced The Machrie on Islay. However, since I visited I read that a Norwegian investment firm from Tromsø has bought a stake in Lofoten with an injection of capital designed for investment in the course and other visitor facilities in the area.

But great golf courses do not suddenly appear; they take time to evolve and for now we should glory on what has already been achieved. Let's start with the setting – there is no more beautiful nor dramatic setting in which to play golf and in June you can play 24 hours a day. The location comes with challenges however, because the climate allows a maximum of five months of golf per year and the weather, always a challenge to greenkeepers the world over, can have a devastating impact on the turf and greens. To some extent you have to start afresh every year. I played in August and the quality of turf was mixed but this in no way compromised the experience.

As there have been so many changes it is difficult to identify the 'old' holes from the new and it is not important. The layout is at times a little eccentric but this does not detract from the experience. Certainly, the start is dramatic; the first hole reminded me immediately of Machrihanish with a drive over the bay to a right to left curving fairway. It is shorter than Machrihanish so big hitters could even try and drive the green but for everyone it is a case of risk and reward as to how much of the bay you cut off. Whatever your decision it requires good control of distance in order not to go too far into a rocky area of rough across the fairway. 'Rocky rough' is a feature of the course and again something you need to accept – links enthusiasts will not be used to facing this hazard. Even if you are successful in finding the tight fairway with your drive, the second shot is very tricky as the green is small. It is a great hole and there is a plan to build the clubhouse high up in the rocks overlooking a back tee.

If the first hole is good, the second is visually extraordinary. This is a new hole and the green is set out on a small rocky promontory surrounded by rocks. You play from a high tee position above the first green and, depending on which tee you use, it is only about 150 yards but the shot is intimidating. If there is a cross wind it is extremely difficult even though the green and its modest surrounds are slightly larger than they look from the tee. I am not sure, however, if it is a particularly good hole and was interested to hear from Jerry the thought about taking the tee box down to sea level to the left-hand side of the first green. I think that might not make it look as dramatic but it might make it a better hole. The third is another wonderful golf hole. The back tee is next to the second green and requires a nearly 200-yard carry across the beach to hit the fairway. Actually, I think the hole is better from the shorter tee where the fairway narrows and dog-legs dramatically at about 200 yards, requiring a very accurate tee shot. If this is successfully negotiated there is a short iron into the green but again, like the 1st, it is small and not easy to hold and there is plenty of trouble with the beach to the left.

The iconic 2nd hole at Lofoten Links – you just have to hope the cross wind isn't too strong

I played the course three times and on my third attempt, I parred the first three holes. I can't tell you how pleased with myself I was. There is a bit of a walk to the 4th tee and the course now heads back inland, crossing the road to the 5th which plays back to the temporary clubhouse. The short 6th is an excellent Par 3, playing uphill to a slightly hidden green. There then follows two successive Par 5s (one will play with the wind and one against) and three Par 4s which lie in the shadow of the Hov mountain. It's not my favourite part of the course though, as you are elevated, the views across the coast are excellent. You cross the road again to 12 which is another glorious Par 3 which plays straight out to sea with an elevated green requiring clever shot-making to hold it. The next section, 13-17 is my favourite as you return to the coast and there is a wide selection of holes which deliver fun to various degrees. Perhaps the most distinctive hole is the 14th which has a Kingsbarns feel to it, hugging the coastline with a narrow fairway which snakes one way and then the other. The 15th is perhaps less distinctive as it plays uphill and inland but I liked it as in my second round I played two 3- woods, my second into the wind sailing over the pin to about 12 feet from where I rolled in a downhill put for my only birdie of my trip. The joy of links golf, the joy of hitting a good shot, the joy of holing the putt for the birdie – every golfer will recognise it. The 17th plays back towards the sea with the shot to the beachside green needing to be fearsomely accurate. 17 is a Par 3 played across some rushes before the 18th returns to the road.

Lofoten Links is now rated as the best course in Norway. I have not played any other courses in Norway so cannot judge but whatever the technical merits of the course this is simply a joyous place to play the game. I think that the course will evolve; there are improvements which could be made as there are with all golf courses, even very old, established ones, and perhaps the routing isn't quite right yet. The condition of the course will never be perfect and perhaps there are at times rocks in places where it would be better not to have them. But if golf is about 'that joy to be alive feeling' then Lofoten must be up there with the best courses in the world. When you play it, it feels a real privilege to be there and somehow its remoteness and the difficulty in getting there add to this feeling.

Covid 19 has delivered some question marks about the future of international travel which won't help Lofoten's cause. But I think perhaps as important for Lofoten is not the international golf tourist but the local, Norwegian one. Maybe Norway has not got a famous golf tradition but Suzann Peterson who memorably holed the final putt on the final green at Gleneagles to win the Solheim Cup for Europe in 2019 has been a well-known name in golf for many years. Now with Viktor Hovland winning the US Amateur in 2018 and since turning professional becoming a Top 10 player in the world surely this will increase the profile of golf within Norway. The news of the new investment and a high profile visit to the course by Victor Hovland (he now unsurprisingly holds the course record) suggests a bright future for this truly extraordinary golfing location.

Afterword

I DON'T WANT this to be a Covid or a Brexit book or one which pontificates on how our politicians should maintain world peace, but it has been hard to write without being influenced by all of these historic events. Much as I was tempted to ignore them, I think they all offer lessons and have relevance. Covid travel restrictions also delayed the publication of this book by some two years.

Whisky and golf have become globalised and it was in this context that I wished to examine how they have developed in Europe. Covid is a reminder of how our world is connected – a virus which seemingly takes hold in one part of the world very quickly spreads and upsets order everywhere. Brexit was caused by a tension between localism and globalism, the challenge of trying to retain local identity while cooperating and being part of a bigger idea. All these are full of contradictions. I won't pronounce on either but I see globalism and international cooperation as positive things while also cherishing diverse cultures and local identities. Is it too much to have both?

Whisky is an interesting example. Scotch Whisky has its own set of rules and parameters – it has a set of values. Many other countries seek broadly to copy these but with their own twist. Seven of the ten biggest whisky brands in the world are Indian whisky brands, but as they are mostly made from molasses as opposed to malted grain, they are not 'whisky' by our definition.

There is nothing wrong with that. Golf is regulated around the world by the R&A and the USPGA which (broadly) agree a common set of rules. I say 'broadly' because there are some very specific differences in the interpretation of these rules both in the professional and the amateur game. For example, on the US PGA Tour a professional can ask for a second opinion on a ruling, something which the European Tour (now called the DP World Tour) does not allow. I was also surprised to find out that in the US when you are playing 'pick and place' (what is sometimes known as 'winter rules') you can place your ball within a club length as opposed to the 6 inches which is permitted in the UK and Europe. You can argue in each case which is the better rule – it doesn't really matter.

My trips around Europe discovering the best of whisky and golf tell me that you can have the best of both worlds. Golf and whisky lend themselves to diversity within a common framework and set of values. Most of the whisky businesses I visited were very wedded to their locality making it central to their marketing ; Armorik in Brittany, Owl in Hesbaye in Belgium, Zuidam in the Netherlands, Puni and Slyrs in their respectively Italian and German Alpine localities, Myken on its remote Norwegian island. However, they all also see themselves as part of a global whisky community.

There is also a global golfing community and within that a range of golf course types, often dictated by local geographical and climatic conditions. I think the best golf courses are those which allow you to play 'the running game' as opposed to 'target golf' but this can be achieved in many different ways. I prefer older links or heathland courses to newer resort courses but that is not to denigrate the latter. I think Scotch Single Malt whiskies (and perhaps also Irish Single Malt and Irish Pot Still whiskey) are the benchmark but the world would be a less interesting place if we did not have newcomers from the likes of Norway and Italy producing similar type products. There is also much debate about golf-course design and different styles from 'heroic' to 'penal' and 'strategic'. Within this, I always think that a good course is one that offers a wide variety of holes and hole types. 18 holes of 'penally' designed golf course doesn't sound much fun to me and watching professionals playing tournaments we want to see both birdies and bogeys plus the occasional eagle and double-bogey. Golf-course architectural trends are moving towards more minimalist and 'natural' designs and greater understanding of the importance of fine grasses in delivering the most enjoyable challenge. I think that Europe is perhaps a little behind the trend on fine grasses as I do think some of the wonderful courses I visited would benefit from more attention to this. With some exceptions, the quality of the course conditions I encountered were generally poorer than I would have expected on a similar tour within the U.K. and Ireland and a predominance of fine grasses was the exception rather than the rule. In some ways the most fun golf I played was at Fanø despite its poor condition but because it was natural links grasses and the running game was the only option. Wonderful layouts like Royal Sart-Tilman in Belgium, while beautifully manicured, would deliver an even more enjoyable challenge if it could make more use of fine grasses. Certainly, Tom Simpson didn't design it for target golf.

Covid has for many been a mental-health challenge as much as a physical health one, and success in golf, like many sports, is as much a mental as a physical pursuit. Coping with the unforeseen and how you react to adversity are challenges for life and golf alike. I am reminded of the final twelve words of Thomas Hardy's *The Mayor of Casterbridge* – 'happiness was but the occasional episode in a general drama of pain'. This perhaps describes many of my rounds of golf.

More philosophically, during lockdown when I was due to be enjoying a round at a particular course, I would consider how I might have played. Would I have got a par at that particularly tricky short hole? Just think of all those shots which exist but were never played. The usual selection: the 5 iron which was surprisingly hit out of the middle and sailed towards the flag; the long, snaking 30-foot putt that somehow you holed; the awkward bunker shot which just cleared the lip and gently rolled to finish within six inches of the pin. There were also of course the duck hook drives which ended in the trees and the topped pitch which skidded over the back of the green into a gorse bush and the missed 18-inch putt which you didn't concentrate on. These are all actual shots which would have been played but have been lost to the world. It's a bit like Mozart's 42nd Symphony and his 28th Piano Concerto. They must exist because if he had lived beyond the disappointingly young age of 37 years he would surely have written them so while these particular combinations of notes do exist, we have lost them forever. Van Gogh also died at just 37 – think of all those paintings of his which he didn't have the chance to paint; masterpieces which we would have had but don't exist. And who would have won The Masters if it had been played in April 2020 or The Open in July of that year? We have missing champions and we will never know who they were.

Covid has taught us all many lessons, some universal and some personal. The effects on our lives have been profound in many ways. We have had to learn new language and terms:

'R numbers', 'self-isolation', 'social distancing' etc. One that intrigued me was the British Government apparently deciding policy on the basis not of 'forecasts' but of what was called a 'realistic worst-case scenario'. This got me thinking; is this something I could apply to my golf? Before deciding on which shot to play, perhaps I should determine the 'realistic worst-case scenario'. This could be particularly useful when there is water about or the pin is situated close to a cavernous bunker, or the out of bounds encroaches into the course. Yet, if I let the 'realistic worst-case scenario' determine every shot I played then I think my golf would become very conservative and certainly my game would be less fun. Maybe there would be fewer disasters but surely also fewer highlights. I think that Jean van de Velde could have benefited from this approach on the 18th tee at Carnoustie in 1999; on the other hand, if Seve had been persuaded by it (unlikely) we would never have witnessed his aforementioned magical shot at Crans-sur-Sierre in 1993.

Covid has in fact been a boost for golf. Golf-club memberships were in decline before the pandemic while recently enquiries to join clubs have risen dramatically. Within clubs, usage of courses has also risen dramatically as members have looked to play golf as their permitted exercise. With many people 'working from home', playing golf midweek has been opened up to many more people which is surely a good thing. I had also hoped that this renewed interest in golf might help speed up the game. In the UK, after the first easing of lockdown, golf was only permitted in pairs so all golf was two-ball singles. To maximise course usage, our course was split into 10 holes and 8 holes (as opposed to two 9s because that's the way it best works). I hugely enjoyed this – the 8-hole loop took about an hour and a quarter, the 10 holes about an hour and a half. I used a pencil bag with about ten clubs in it. It was good exercise and great fun – isn't that what golf is meant to be?

As courses struggle with capacity, the default position is to allow only four-ball golf. The contention is that it maximises the number of people who can play. Of course, the way of allowing the maximum number of people to play is to have a day of foursomes – the speed of play (if it is played properly) will be significantly quicker and allow about 30% more players to use the course in any given time period – they will just play a little less golf. It is a controversial subject as many golfers really don't like or understand foursomes which is, in my opinion, a shame. Golf as an individual sport, where you are constantly striving for self-improvement, is good but golf as a team sport can also be enormously rewarding. I am struck when playing medals with some people how self-absorbed they can be. In the bar after the round, they can talk you through all the ups and downs of their round without any thought as to how their playing partners have fared. It was them against the course. This is how medal play is set up. The same is true with the professionals; they are totally focused on their own game. I was amused to hear from a tournament referee that when Covid protocols for scoring in professional tournaments changed and professionals were required to mark their own cards, there were many fewer mistakes when the scores were confirmed. The old system where professional A marked professional B's card apparently often brought about frequent errors because professional A had no interest whatsoever in professional B's score and so took little care. When professionals mark their own scorecard they make sure that they get it right.

Foursomes is in my view a loftier pursuit that decries self-absorption. I have wanted to talk about hubris and arrogance which are in my view two particularly unattractive human characteristics which we all come across in many walks of life – I certainly did in my business career. Politicians and some international statesmen are, I'm afraid, another example. We have found during the Covid crisis that even some scientists suffer from these shortcomings. Many would pronounce that it was perfectly obvious what needed doing (without having to take responsibility for the doing) while others were more ready to admit that in fact we were dealing with a lot of unknowns and making the right decisions was very difficult. I would suggest that the latter would make better golfers and makers of whisky. There is a fine line between self-confidence and hubris and arrogance and I think golf is good at exposing that line. Many in business who have experienced success assume that this success is down to their own peculiar talent when very often that talent has been supplemented by a large slice of luck. They assume that every deal they touch will turn to gold. A golfer should always recognise that a run of birdies will usually be a combination of good shot-playing and a measure of luck and golfers with the humility to recognise this will in the long term be the better for it. Foursomes golf in particular brings this home. The whisky making process is also a combination of art and science with sometimes unpredictable results and those that recognise this are the better for it.

While Covid has clearly affected short term business plans of many whisky distilleries – because, to some extent, it is a product which, by its nature, has a long-term outlook – the effect of Covid will be more limited. Distillery visits were suspended for much of 2020 and to many businesses this was an important source of income, though perhaps less so in Europe than in Scotland. Tariff issues are a bigger concern though again these will have impacted Scotch Malt Whisky brands where the US export market had become significantly larger than European ones. But even tariff disputes are relatively short-term disruptions; one has to believe that sense will prevail.

So, while 2020 to 2022 provided an enormous and uncomfortable jolt to the rhythm of life it also offered a number of lessons: that we do not know what lies ahead and so we need to be able to accept and adapt and acknowledge that often there is no right answer. Let me extol the virtues of nuance; life is complicated and there are many ways of facing it. Our politicians and scientists should accept that even within their respective parameters of political values and scientific facts, there is always nuance as to what the right answer is. It's the same with golf; if you are 150 yards from the green it may usually be a 6 iron but sometimes a 5 or a 7 would in fact work better for a whole host of reasons. Sometimes it is right to take on a risky shot and go for the flag but equally playing short and hoping for a straightforward chip and a putt can also be the right decision. With whisky, there are some fundamental principles of distilling and maturing but there are also many nuances in both processes which can make significant differences. And none is right and none is wrong. They are just different and we should embrace this. Across the continent I have encountered both a love and respect for the core values of golf and whisky but also an incredible diversity in types of golf courses and clubs and diversity of approach to the minutiae of whisky making. This is how it should be and, I hope, how it will continue to be.

I would therefore commend both whisky and golf as examples of pastimes which point to how we can live better lives in a better world. The world seems to have become, with the aid of social media, a much 'shoutier' place with less understanding of the value of courtesy and respect. Golf is not a 'shouty' sport and whisky is not a 'shouty' drink. Golf is a sport where the values of fair play and 'playing the ball as it lies' are engrained as are the rules of etiquette, treating your opponent with the same respect. Good manners should not go out of fashion. Whisky is one of few products which does not conform to modern business norms of just-in-time supply chains and manufacturing cost efficiency. No other branded products owned by multi-national companies would be manufactured at so many geographically remote sites. There are rules for making whisky but its values are more important. There is no such thing as the best whisky.

I started with my own maxim, *Expect the unexpected,* and I will end with one from a rather more eminent literary figure, Victor Hugo, who wrote: *Nothing is more imminent than the impossible… what we must always foresee is the unforeseen.* If Covid has taught us to deal with the unexpected and forced us to adapt and always search for improvement, then this is an approach to both the playing of golf and the making of whisky which I would commend.

Bibliography

While there are numerous fine books on both whisky and golf the following were particularly relevant to this book

Malt Whisky	Charles MacLean	**Lomond Books 2013**
Whiskey A Global History	Kevin R Kosar	**Reaktion Books 2016**
Maclean's Miscellany of Whisky	Charles MacLean	**Little Books Ltd. 2015**
The World Atlas of History	Dave Broom	**Hachette 2014**
Malt Whisky Yearbook 2022		**MagDig Media 2021**
Whisky	Aeneas Macdonald	**Birlinn 2016**
A Field Guide to Whisky	Hans Offringa	**Artisan 2017**
The Philosophy of Whisky	Billy Abbott	**The British Library 2021**
The Links	Robert Hunter	**Coventry House 2018**
The 100 Greatest Ever Golfers	Andy Farrell	**Elliott & Thompson 2011**
The Spirit of St Andrews	Alister MacKenzie	**Broadway Books**
Methods of early golf architecture	The selected writings of Alister MacKenzie, H.S Colt and A. W. Tillinghast	**Coventry House 2013**

BV - #0141 - 091222 - C27 - 190/133/11 - CC - 9781914424816 - Gloss Lamination